CHILEAN POETS

CHILEAN POETS
A NEW ANTHOLOGY

Edited by JORGE ETCHEVERRY

MARICK PRESS

Library of Congress Cataloguing in Publication Data

CHILEAN POETS: A NEW ANTHOLOGY
English translations copyright Marick Press
English translations copyright Jorge Etcheverry
ISBN: 978-1-934851-24-1
Copyright © by Marick Press, 2011
Design and typesetting by Alison Carr
Cover design by Marick Press
Cover image: Jorge Etcheverry
Printed and bound in the United States

Marick Press
P.O. Box 36253
Grosse Pointe Farms
Michigan 48236
www.marickpress.com

Distributed by spdbooks.org
And In**gram**

INTRODUCTION BY JORGE ETCHEVERRY

INTRODUCTION

To do an anthology, any kind of anthology, is a risky business. Anthologizing works from a specific country multiplies these risks. You cannot attempt an exhaustive collection—there will always be poets that are not included—the criteria of literary quality and poetic relevance of one kind or another varies from generation to generation, and they are different according to different social and cultural groups. In the end, an anthology is a representation of the social and cultural background of the editor, his/her ideology and preferences, and the degree of awareness he/she has of the literary institution or his/her connections with it. At the very most, the editor can work within historical currents and make a pact with relativity.

An anthology of Chilean poetry must include the indisputable classics, Pablo Neruda, Gabriela Mistral, Pablo de Rokha, Vicente Huidobro and Nicanor Parra. Regarding the numerous other voices of Chilean poetry, we have preferred to provide a sampling that at times showcases the most representative or common characteristics of a group or generation, and at other times presents the most outstanding voices in terms of their critical reception (bearing in mind that critical reception is always relative and depends on current trends and books markets). This anthology also gives considerable space to new, or relatively new, voices within the many branches of contemporary Chilean poetry. In some cases, we have not restricted ourselves exclusively to the best-known poets or poems, or to the preferences of established critics: we have selected some of the better known poets of different generations and orientations alongside others that we considered particularly remarkable or representative of diverse perspectives and aesthetic/thematic considerations. So, in this venture, we have included poets from different periods, regions, generations and sensibilities of contemporary Chilean poetry, which we hope will give readers a sense of the rich variety of this body of work.

Chilean poetry can be considered a result of the productive tension between opposing trends or contradictory appeals; the permanent conflict between established conventions and the new; between the urban center and its tributary regions; between continuity and change; between the need for meaning, content, and value and linguistic rupture and exploration; between the geographical, physical country and its diaspora; between commercial publication and insertion in the market of goods and commodities, and the marginal initiatives; between *avant garde* adventures at the limits of language and the craving for simple, universal communication. This, as the critic Soledad Bianchi has expressed, has resulted in "tanta y tan variada poesía" [so much and such diverse poetry], in which coexist practically all possible kinds of poetry in the Spanish language. This sometimes produces a pluridiscursivity and pluritextuality within a single poem—a complexity that does not however cloud the poem's meaning, as can be seen in some of the works compiled here.

Like many other national literatures, Chilean poetry no longer has a unique canon that establishes the universal rules for writing, and it now displays a limitless variety and richness of form and content. This is due to a number of factors, including the massive exile of Chilean writers (and of an important part of the Chilean literary institution) after the 1973 coup d'état, which gave rise to the subsequent literary diaspora. In the case of this book, those authors that represent the Chilean poetic diaspora are mainly from the North American sphere, particularly Canada and the US, and we have chosen to showcase a combination of new and established Chilean voices from this region. Thus, Chilean poets living outside of Chile are an important presence in this anthology.

Like their counterparts in Chile, these poets display many formal and thematic orientations, and some are more experienced poetic voices while others are still in development. The writing from this geographical and cultural area has proven to be particularly rich for Chile's literary and poetic diaspora. This branch of Chilean poetry offers unique versions of the subjects of exile and dislocation, nostalgia, assimilation, political commitment, denunciation, and alienation. Among the different glimpses provided in this anthology, there are texts with the classic subjects and formats we now expect from the poetry of exile and migration, such as uprootedness, nostalgia, and comparisons between the home and host societies and cultures. Yet, the work of these poets also illustrates the thematic and formal hybridizations of Chilean poetry produced outside of the country, which in some cases has incorporated cultural and linguistic elements of their host countries. Such themes and stylistic experimentation, of course, are not entirely new to the Chilean poetic kaleidoscope since Mistral, Neruda, and Huidobro were themselves exiled or transplanted poets who produced major works during their time abroad. Hence, Chilean diasporic poetry also incorporates elements of the diverse, ubiquitous and polydiscursive fresco of Chilean poetry, which constitutes a sort of alternative world that reflects the instances and history of Chile's national life inside and outside its borders.

Another major socio-historical shift that has altered the terrain of many national literatures—including Chile's—is the advent of globalization. The identity politics associated with the "First world," for example, have spread throughout much of the so-called developing world, including Latin America, where they have resonated widely where the social and cultural conditions for such politics were already deeply entrenched. In the last decades, the processes of gender, ethnic, community and linguistic validation (and recognition) already underway in the literatures of the First World— for instance the development of gay, feminist, Native and ethnic literatures— have been readily incorporated into already existing tendencies, branches and *regroupements* of Chilean literature. So, nowadays, some poetry and poets become, or are considered to be, representatives of these particular social or cultural groups whereas Chilean poets in the 1960s were generally grouped by their different ways of conceptualizing and writing poetry, as well as through geographical distinctions. Virtual media and ICTs have also shifted the shape, territory and parameters of "national" literatures, making it difficult for the national to refer exclusively to what is written inside the physical borders of any given country. We have, for these reasons, chosen to include young authors from the 'inside' of the country along with both new and more or less established voices from the so-called 'diaspora.' Many of these can be considered emerging voices that in some instances signal a renewal or potential promise in the realm of poetry.

The internationalization of Chilean literature and poetry has been accentuated by the reality of globalization with its massive and diverse migrations and displacements. Chilean poetry has acquired a planetary presence since the almost massive exodus of poets after 1973, their partial return, and the poetic resistance inside the country that established communications with poets outside (and which continues today). The influence of this global reality on the future of this "enormous impure animal" that is Chilean poetry (as it somnolently digests this variegated food) is difficult to discern—at least by me. Let us finish, then, with a moment of encounter in a faraway urban setting, which becomes alive and substantial in the words of a Chilean poet who, until recently, lived in Sweden:

FIREFLIES

Carlos Geywitz

I see her there,
giving her face to the window,
with no makeup other
than her vacant eyes.
I move closer,
ask her for the last cigarette
and notice the imperfect line of her lips.
Just in passing
Her expression suggests
stories of fading passengers.
The pulse of this
night
threatens to scratch
the walls of my heart.
We leave the bar, we go out, luminous
to love each other,
to interchange anguish
knowing that dawn is inexorable.

Translated by Jorge Etcheverry, edited by Sharon Khan
Noviembre de 2009

GABRIELA MISTRAL

TO SEE HIM AGAIN

And never, never again?
Not on nights filled with quivering stars,
or during dawn's maiden brightness
or sacrificed afternoons?

Or at the edge of a pale road
that encircles the farmlands,
or upon the rim of a trembling fountain,
whitened by a moon?

Or beneath the forest's
luxuriant, raveled tresses
where, calling him,
I was overtaken by the night
Neither in the grotto that returns
the echo of my cry?

Oh no. To see him again —
it would not matter where —
in heaven's dead water
or inside the boiling vortex,
or under serene moons or in bloodless fright!

To be with him...
to be every springtime and winters,
united in one anguished knot
around his bloody neck!

Version by Mariela Griffor

VÍCTOR JARA

PRAYER TO A FARM WORKER

Rise up and look at the mountain, from
where the wind, the sun, the water come.
Thou, who determines the course of
rivers, thou who scatters the flight of
your soul.
Rise up and look at your hands. Join
hands with your brothers to grow, together
united in blood we go. Now is the time that
can be tomorrow.
Deliver us from the one that keep us
in misery. Take us to your kingdom of justice and
equality. Blow like the wind the gorge's flower.
Clean like fire
the barrel of my gun.
Thy will be done
here on Earth. Give us your strength and
your courage in combat.
Blow like the wind the gorge's flower.
Clean like fire the barrel of my gun.

Rise up and look at your hands. Join
hands with your brothers to grow, together
united in blood we go,
now and at the hour of
our death. Amen. Amen.

Version by Mariela Griffor

ENRIQUE LIHN

TORTURE CHAMBER

Your help is my compensation
Your compensation is the quadrature of my circle
Which removes with its fingers in order to maintain its agility
Your calculator is my hand which is missing a finger
with which I avoid calculation errors
your charity is the capital I use when I ask for it

Your appearance in the open air mall Ahumada

it is my debut in society
His society is secret in regards to my tribe
His personal security is my lack of decision
His kerchief in the pocket is my white flag
His tie is my Gordian knot
His Falabella suit is my velvet curtain
His right shoe is my left shoe
.... twelve years later
The crease of his pants is the limit
That I could not cross
Not even if I could disguise myself as you
after I force you to undress
His climb of the stairs of the Bank of Chile
Is my dream of Jacob through which a blond angel descends
and of painted wings to pay,
body to body, all my debt
His wallet is my sack of papers
when I get high
His signature is my entertainment of an illiterate
His two plus two is four is my two minus two

His going and coming is my labyrinth
en which I growling loose myself persecuted
by a fly
His office is the inner lining where one can be condemned to death
my name and his trespass to another cadaver
………………………….that takes it to a friendly country
His clinic is my torture chamber
His torture chamber
is the only hotel
where you can get in at any time
……………………………..without forewarning on his part
His mandate is my singing
His electric pen is what makes me
a productive author one illuminated cursed
…………………………….or a arrogant that cowers
it depends who I am at that moment
His bad mood is my blood
His kick in the butt is my rising
to the heavens that are what they are
………….and, God forbid
His tranquility is my death stab in the back
His liberty is my everlasting
His peace is my peace
…………………….of course if I can enjoy it
eternally and yours for life
His real life is the end of my imagination
……………………………..when I get high
His wife is in that case my burst cat
His toothpick is now my fork
His fork is my spoon
His knife is my temptation to cut his throat
……………………….…..when I get high
His policeman is the guardian of my impropriety
His shepherd is my executioner

at the door of his house as if I was not
.... cursed lost lamb
His submachine gun is my bride that I lie with in dreams
His helmet is the form
in which they pour in the head of my newborn child
His outhouse is my nuptial march
His garbage is my pantheon
..........................as long as they don't take
the cadavers.

Version by Mariela Griffor

MUD

Mud, unending malice. All other sources gives up at last
To the pressure of this primal matter.
The days of water are numbered, but not the mud's
That packs up after the well is plugged.
Not the mud's days that backs up to the seventh day of the Creation.

As children we played with it, it is not strange it plays with us,
Shaped after its image and likeness.

II

God the father, God the Son, God the Holy Ghost:
Land and water, then, the original mud.
A single sentiment at the beginning of it all:
This unendless rancor.

III

Sooner or later we will come to our senses.
It is the way of things; we don't get to know them till
      we take them more or less calmly,
as if nothing had happened.

IV

The real stranger is oneself. The looks of some other
      who ended up haunting us,
for finally accepting one of many invitations.
I thought I saw my shadow when I opened the door,
      just as we were about to go out.
The function had begun. "Come in. come in."
"We were waiting for you" I said and she said,
      "I don't recognize ingratitude"
With a curious tremor in her voice.

Version by Mariela Griffor

NICANOR PARRA

THE PILGRIM

Your attention, ladies and gentleman, your attention for one
    moment:
Turn your heads for a second to this part of the republic.
Forget for one night your personal affairs,
Pleasure and pain can wait at the door:
There's a voice from this part of the republic.
Your attention, ladies and gentlemen! You attention for one
    moment!
A soul that has been bottled up for years
In a sort of sexual and intellectual abyss,
Nourishing itself most inadequately through the nose,
Desires to be heard.
I'd like to find out some things,
I need a little light, the garden's covered with flies,
My mental state's a disaster,
I work things out in my particular way,
As I say these things I see bicycle leaning against a wall,
I see a bridge
And a car disappearing between the buildings.

You comb your hair, that's true, you walk in the gardens,
Under your skins you have other skins,
You have a seventh sense
Which lets you in and out automatically.
But I'm a child calling to its mother from behind rocks,
I'm a pilgrim who makes stones jump as high as his nose,
A tree crying out to be covered with leaves.

Version by Mariela Griffor

THE TABLETS

I dreamed I was in a desert and I was sick of myself then
I started beating a woman.
It was devilish cold, I had to do something,
Make a fire, take some exercise,
But I had a headache, I was tired,
All I wanted to do was sleep, die.
My suit was soggy with blood
And a few hairs were stuck among my fingers
-They belonged to my poor mother
"Why do you abuse your mother," a stone asked me,
A dusty stone, "Why do you abuse her?"
I couldn't tell where these voices came from, they gave me the shivers,
I looked at my nails, I bit them,
I tried to think of something but without success,
All I saw around me was a desert
And the image of that idol
My god who was watching me do these things.
Then a few birds appeared
And at the same moment, in the dark, I discovered some slabs of rock.
With a supreme effort I managed to make out the tablets of the law:
"We are the tablets of the law," they said,
"Why do you abuse your mother?
See these birds that have come to perch on us,
They are here to record your crimes."
But I yawned, I was bored with these warnings.
"Get rid of those birds," I said aloud.
"No," one of the stones said,
"They stand for your different sins,
They're here to watch you."
So I turned back to my lady again
And started to let her have it harder than before.
I had to do something to keep awake.

I had no choice but to act
Or I would have fallen asleep among those rocks
And those birds.
So I took a box of matches out of one of my pockets
And decided to set fire to the bust of the god.
I was dreadfully cold, I had to get warm,
But that blaze only lasted a few seconds.
Out of my mind, I looked for the tablets again
But they had disappeared.
The rocks weren't there either.
My mother had abandoned me.
I beat my brow. But
There was nothing more I could do.

Version by Mariela Griffor

THE VIPER

For years I was condemned to worship a
despicable woman
Sacrifice myself for her, endure endless humiliations
and mockery,
Work night and day to feed her and clothe her,
Perform several crimes, commit several misdemeanors,
Practice petty burglary by moonlight,
Forge compromising documents,
For fear of a scornful glance from her fascinating eyes.
During brief phases of understanding we used to meet
      In parks
And photographed together driving
        a motorboat,
Or we would go to a nightclub
And fling ourselves into an orgy of dancing
That went on until very late at night.
Long years I was under the spell of that woman
Who used to appear in my office completely naked
 performing contortions that defy the imagination,
Simply to draw my poor soul into her orbit
And above all to wring from me my last penny.
She strictly forbade me to have anything to do with
      my family.
my friends were separated from me with defamatory libels
Which this viper published in a newspaper she owned.
Passionate to the point of delirium, she never let up for
      an moment,
Commanding me to kiss her on the mouth
replying at once to her silly questions
Concerning, among other things, eternity and the afterlife,
Subjects which upset me to a terribly sad state,
Producing buzzing in my ears, recurrent nausea, sudden

fainting spells
Which she turned to account with that practical turn of
	mind that distinguished her,
Putting her clothes on without wasting a moment
And clearing out of my apartment, leaving me atonished.

This situation dragged on for five years and more.
There were periods when we lived together in a
	round room
In a luxurious district near the cemetery, sharing the rent.
(Some nights we had to interrupt our honeymoon
to deal with the rats that came in through the
	window.)
The viper kept detailed records
In which she noted every penny I borrowed from her,
She would not let me use the toothbrush I gave
	her myself,
and she accused me of ruining her youth:
with eyes flashing fire she threatened to take me
to court
And make me pay what I owed her as soon as
	possible
since she needed the money to continue her studies.
Then I had to take to the streets and live on charity,
Sleeping on park benches
Where the police found me time and again, dying,
among the first leaves of autumn.
Fortunately that situation didn't last long,
For on time—and again I was in a park,
Posing for a photographer—
A pair of delicious feminine hands suddenly covered
	my eyes
While a voice that I loved asked me: Who am I.
You are my love, I answered serenely.

My angel! She said nervously.
Let me sit on your knees once again!
It was then that I was able to ponder the fact that she was
    Now wearing thongs.

It was a memorable meeting, though full of discordant
    notes.
I have bought a piece of land not far from the
    Slaughterhouse, she exclaimed.
I plan to build a sort of pyramid there
where we can spend the rest of our days.
I have finished my studies; I have been admitted to the bar,
I have capital at my disposal;
Let's go into some lucrative business, we two, my love,
    she added,
Let's build our nest far from the world.
Enough of your stupidities, I answered, I have no
    confidence in your plans.
think that my real wife
Can at any moment leave both of us in the most
    frightful poverty.
My children are grown up, time has elapsed,
I feel utterly exhausted; let me have a minutes rest,
Get me a little water, woman,
Get me something to eat from somewhere,
I'm starving,
I can't work for you any more,
It's over between us.

Version by Mariela Griffor

WALKING AROUND

It so happens I'm tired of being a man.
I go into the tailor shops and the movies
all shriveled up, impenetrable, like a wooly swan
navigating on a ocean of origin and ash.

The smell of barber shops makes me cry out loud.
I only want a rest from stones or from wool,
from not seeing buildings or gardens,
or merchandise, or eyeglasses, or elevators.

I am tired of my feet and my nails
and my hair and my shadow.
I am tired of being a man.

Still it would be delicious
to scare a notary public with a cut lily
or kill a nun with a hit in the ear.
It would be nice
just to walk down the streets with a green knife
screaming until I freeze to death.

I won't like to continue to go on being a root in the dark,
hesitating, stretched out, shivering in my sleep,
deep down, in the wet gut of the universe,
soaking and thinking, eating every day.

I don't want misfortunes.
I won't have it this way, being a root and a tomb,
in a alone underground, in a cellar with terrifying corpses,

Cold, dying of sadness.

That's why Monday burns like oil
when it sees me arrive with my prisoner's face,
or squeaks like a broken-down wheel as it goes
stepping hot-blooded into the night.

And it shoves me along to certain corners, to certain damp houses,
to hospitals where the bones hang out the windows,
to certain cobblers' shops smelling of vinegar,
to streets horrendous like cervices.

There are sulfur-colored birds and horrible intestines
hanging on the doors of the houses I hate,
there are sets of false teeth forgotten in a coffee-pot,
there are mirrors
which should have wept with shame and horror,
there are umbrellas all over the place, and poisons, and belly buttons.

I walk along with calm, with eyes, with shoes,
with fury, with forgetfulness,
I pass, I cross offices and surgical stores
and courtyards where clothes hang from wire:
underwear, towels and shirts that weep
slowly dribbling dirty tears.

Version by Mariela Griffor

BODY OF A WOMAN

Body of a woman, white hills, white thighs,
you are like the world in your attitude of surrender.
My wild farm worker's body digs in you
and makes the son leap from the depth of the earth.

I was alone like a tunnel. The birds fled from me,
and night swamped me with its powerful invasion.
To survive myself I forged you like a weapon,
like an arrow in my bow, a stone in my sling.

But the hour of vengeance falls, and I love you.
Body of skin, of moss, of eager and firm milk.
Of the goblets of the breast! Oh the eyes of absence!
Oh the roses of the pubis! Oh your voice, slow and sad!

Body of my woman, I will persist in your grace.
My thirst, my boundless desire, my shifting road!
Dark river-beds where the eternal thirst flows
and weariness follows, and the infinite pain.

Version by Mariela Griffor

TONIGHT I CAN WRITE...

Tonight I can write the saddest lines.

Write, for example, "The night is shattered
and the blue stars shiver at the distance."

The night wind revolves in the sky and sings.

Tonight I can write the saddest lines.
I loved her, and sometime she loved me too.

Through nights like this one I held her in my arms.
I kissed her again and again under the infinite sky.

She loved me, sometimes I loved her too.
How could one not have loved her great still eyes.

Tonight I can write the saddest lines.
To think that I do not have her. To feel I have lost her.

To hear the immense night, still more immense without her.
And the verse falls to the soul like dew to the pasture.

What does it matter that my love could not keep her.
The night is shattered and she is not with me.

This is all. In the distance someone is singing. In the
Distance.
My soul is not satisfied that it has lost her.

My sight searches for her as though to go to her.
My hear looks for her, and she is not with me.

The same night whitening the same trees.
We, of that time, are no longer the same.

I no longer love her, that's certain, but how I loved her.
My voice tried to find the wind to touch her hearing.

Another's. She will be another's. Like my kisses before.
Her voice. Her bright body. Her infinite eyes.

I no longer love her, that's certain, but maybe I love her.
Love is so short, forgetting is so long.

Because through nights like this one I held her in my arms
my soul is not satisfied that it has lost her.

Though this be the last pain that she makes me suffer
and these are the last verses that I write for her.

Version by Mariela Griffor

MAN

Emerged from the luke warm waters
From maternal waters
To travel to frozen
final waters

To the final waters
Of dread
Hidden ports whose newborn
Are all dead.

Version by Mariela Griffor

RAÚL ZURITA

THE SEA
strange baits rain from the sky. Surprising bait falls upon the sea. Down below the ocean, up above unusual clouds on a clear day. Surprising baits rain on the sea. There was a love raining, there was a clear day that's raining now on the sea.

They are shadows, bait for fishes. A clear day is raining, a love that was never said. Love, ah yes, love, amazing baits are raining from the sky on the shadow of fishes in the sea.

Clear days fall. Some strange baits with clear days stuck to them, with loves that were never said.

The sea, it says the sea. It says baits that rain and clear days stuck to them, it says unfinished loves, clear and unfinished days that rain for the fish in the sea.

You can hear whole days sinking, strange sunny mornings, unfinished loves, goodbyes cut short that sink into the sea. You can hear surprising baits that rain with sunny days stuck to them, loves cut short, goodbyes that not any more. Baits are told of, that rain for the fish in the sea.

The blue brilliant sea. You can hear shoals of fish devouring baits stuck with words that not, days and news that not, loves that not any more. It is told of shoals of fish that leap, of whole whirlwinds of fish that leap.

You can hear the sky. It is told that amazing baits rain down with pieces of sky stuck to them upon the sea.

I heard a sea and a sky hallucinated, I heard suns exploding with love fall like fruits, I heard whirlwinds of fish devouring the pink flesh of surprising baits.

I heard millions of fish which are tombs with pieces of sky inside, with hundreds of words that were never said, with hundreds of flowers of red flesh and pieces of sky in the eyes. I heard hundreds of loves that were stopped on a sunny day. Baits rained from the sky.

Viviana cries. Viviana heard whirlwinds of fishes rise up in the air fighting for mouthfuls of a goodbye cut short, of a prayer not heard, of a love not said. Viviana is on the beach. Viviana today is Chile.

The long fish that is Chile rises up through the air devouring the sun baits of its dead.

Tremendous plains rain down for the fishes: days that will now never be, eyes stuck to a final sky, loves that were not said. It says tremendous plains made of arms that couldn't embrace, of hands that didn't touch. It says strange fruits that the fish devour, that the silver tombs which are the fish devour. I heard extraordinary plains raining on the sea.

Extraordinary skies, days, dreams sinking into the silver whirlpools of waves, I heard the silver mouths of fish devouring unfinished goodbyes. I heard immense plains of love saying that no more. Angels, musical scores of love saying no more.

Universes, cosmoses, unfinished winds raining down in thousands of pink baits onto the carnivorous sea of Chile. I heard plains of love never said, infinite skies of love sinking into the carnivorous tombs of the fish.

Here is the sea, it says, the carnivorous tombs of the fish. Here is the almond-coloured flesh and the sea. The sea weeps. Viviana weeps.

There are infinite skies of almond trees, of stars, like fruits they say and fall. Surprising baits fall from the sky like the stars, like fruits that fall on the grass. There are endless universes in the fishes' stomachs, stars, almond orchards. Viviana hears immense orchards of blood-red almond trees falling onto the sea. Infinite clear days raining on the red foam of the sea.

People rain down and fall in strange positions like rare fruit of a strange harvest.

Viviana hears surprising human baits raining down, amazing human fruit harvested in strange fields. Viviana is now Chile. She hears human fruit raining down like golden suns exploding on the waters.

Amazing harvests rained out of the sky. Incredible ripe fruit onto the ploughed fields of the sea. Viviana hears mute silhouettes fall, minutes that did not finish, sacred crosses that rain like clouds onto the waves of the Pacific. She hears torsos, strange mists coming off the waves, strange clouds of soft flesh against the empty sky of the ocean.

Baits rain down with mouthless angels, with scores that could not be heard, with soundless shadows that kiss. Amazing harvests rain down, fall down, extraordinary trees that fall burning into the waves.

Ploughed fields, sacred lands rain from the sky with broken backs, pieces of necks that weren't there any more, unexpected clouds of unending spring. They were thrown. They rain down. Amazing harvests of men come down as food for the fish in the sea. Viviana hears sacred lands rain down, hears her son fall like a cloud onto the unclouded cross of the Pacific.

Crosses made of fish for the Christs. The arch of the Chilean sky falls on the bloody tombs of Christ for the fishes. That's your mother, there. That's your son. Shadows fall on the sea. Strange human baits fall on the crosses of fish in the sea. Viviana wants to cradle fishes in her arms, wants to hear that clear day, that love cut short, that fixed sky. Viviana is now Chile. She cradles fish under the sky that shouts hosanna.

Surprising Christs fall in strange positions onto the crosses of the sea. Surprising baits rain from the sky: a last prayer rains, a last passion, a last day under the sky's hosannas. Infinite skies fall in strange positions onto the sea.

Infinite skies fall, infinite skies of broken legs, of arms bent against the neck, of heads wrenched against backs. Skies weep downwards falling in broken poses, in clouds of broken backs and broken skies. They fall, they sing.

That's your mother, there. That's your son.

That's your son. Viviana hears the arches of eyebrows incredibly raised, hears eyes endlessly open falling from the sky's eyebrows. Hears the nails sinking into the cross of the ocean. The whole Chilean sea is the cross. Infinite plains sing from the sky the hosanna of the cross which is the sea, of the food which falls like plains, like pieces of bread into the sacred stomach of the fish. Viviana hears infinite sacred shoals emerging, infinite fish singing with a voice taken from the sky. The fish go up into the sky. Surprising baits rained down with surprising days, with images of almond trees, with loves cut short. Surprising baits rained on the sacred sea, on the sacred fish.

The sea is holy, holy the wide plains of human fruits that fall, the fish holy. I heard infinite days falling, bodies that fell with skies, with fields glimpsed between them, with trees like a chorus of crosses that sang out in song-sung waters.

Viviana cradles the holy sea. Viviana says somewhere in these sacred waters is her son.

Holy skies rained down. Infinities of water like sons of the holy sky, yes, like pieces of bread, like holy baits beneath the ocean cross of Chile. They wept, rained down sons of loves that never more, of endless meadows that fell in flames, of bushes that burn and do not burn up. Viviana hears whole skies fall like almond trees in flower, like pink cheeks in flower on the redeemed sea of Chile.

The bush that is the Chilean sea burns and does not burn up.

The holy plains of the sky burn falling. Human baits fall onto the flaming bush of the ocean. The fish swim up singing with the voice of the sky, shoals, infinities of fish rise up from the sacred waters.

Strange suns sing raining from the sky, strange fruits on the sacred ocean.

Fish in flames leap, amazing baits burn in the sea. Holy skies rained. Bushes of Chile, there are your sons. Bushes of Chile, there is the sea in flames.

See there the sea burning. Viviana hears skies burning among the flames of the sea, bushes that don't burn up, sons of amazing bushes that burn without being consumed among the flaming waves. Strange days burn falling on the sea, amazing sacred baits that fall and sing upon the burnt pastures of the sea. Viviana is today Chile. She hears songs emerge from the flames on the water, she hears the sacred sky burning with love upon the burning breakers. She hears the INRI of her love rise burning on the burning meadows of the Pacific.

She hears the INRI of the skies burning. Oceans and seas of Chile hear the INRI of the skies burning.

Surprising rose-blood baits rained from strange clouds over the sea, surprising incense-coloured seas rise now singing with the bait of the fish in the sky.

Listen to the song of the fish rising to the sky. Burning, the sacred ocean of Chile burning. Flames like incense tinge with blood and rose the burnt meadows of the Pacific.
Seas

Were thrown. Heavy with strange seed, ploughed fields cover the sea.
Translated by William Rowe

MARJORIE AGOSÍN

YOUR LANGUAGE

Because I love you
I learn your language
Slowly, I repeat
The first syllables
I whistle among the lines
The beginning Aleph
That holds everything

I weave your language while I love you
You teach me to say "your hair still finds a home in the wind"
Skillful, you seal my mouth
With a kiss that resembles the light of silence

I am Penelope in the Holy Land
I learn your language
You kiss me in that language
After seventeen centuries
I love you in it
You make me fill complete.

SEVENTEEN CENTURIES

I learn to make love
In an ancient language
That for seventeen centuries nobody used
To make love
Today the alphabet goes bare

In my tongue
While I love you I learn to decipher
God's words as they used to do it
In the Sidur
Facing a darkened synagogue filled with dark men

I learn to make love in the light
Your mouth teaches me new words
Joyfully, I repeat them just as you repeat a kiss
The skin exhausted after desire

We speak in Hebrew
As if it were God's will
And I learn to name the stars
The signs of pleasure
My body is a crimson alphabet
You take it in your hands
You write with me
I am your word

AFTER THE RAIN

I shall return after the rains
When Jerusalem's sun opens the wound
Agile descending to rest
Next to its stones
I shall anoint my cheeks with them
Those ancient ones, those that furiously
Defied the pain of nostalgia
And I shall feel the urgency of all returns

I shall return after the rains

When winter warms the pink
Stones of Jerusalem
Like you warm me
The sun shall descend softly like a clear fog

And you shall return to me
Like the poppies of the valley
After the rains

POEMAS PARA PAPÁ

I.
More than believing in God,
My father believed in men and in the word
That he shared with humble nobility
He was sparse in his words
And generous in his loves
The day of his death
Hebrew prayers were with him
His body turned to stone
Or memory
Maybe he concluded his wanderings and diasporas
He returned to the root of language
Clear seed in the diaphanous roundness of the earth

II.
The day you died
Somebody let go of
My hand
Let me fall into the abyss
Somebody attacked my faith
Nobody was next to me

Like an orphan child
I wanted to find
The vertigo of emptiness
I did not want to have a history nor
A beginning
Because when you went away
You left me without myself
Wounded I also fell into the precipice of that night
Where death did not grant me consolation nor refuge.

III.
He is not here
He shall not return
He is gone
The piano was left sealed
Night remained even darker
Nothing is
Everything is

Translated by Laura Rocha Nakazawa

ELICURA CHIHUAILAF NAHUELPÁN

THE SPIRITS OF WATER CARRY ME AWAY BLUE DREAM

The blue house where I was born in
   Is placed on a hill
surrounded by *walles*, a willow
    chestnuts, walnuts
a springlike acacia in winter
-a sun with the sweetness of *ulmo* honey-

chilco flowers surrounded by hummingbirds
so fleeting we wondered whether they
  were reality or illusion
In winter we heard the crashing of oaks
   split by lightning
In the evenings we used to go out into the rain, or under
   red clouds, to look for the sheep
(at times we had to mourn the death
   of one of them, sailing over
   the waters)

At night around the hearth we listened
   to songs, stories and riddles
inhaling the fragrance of bread
baked by my grandmother, my mother
   or aunt María
while my father and my grandfather
   -Chief of the community-
gazed with attention and respect
I am not speaking of an idyllic society but
   of memories from my childhood
There, it seems, I learned what

      poetry was
The grandeur of everyday life
and above all its details
the brightness of firelight, of eyes, of
      hands

Seated on my grandmother's lap I first
    heard the stories of trees
and stones that talk to animals
to humans and to one another
All you need, she used to say, is to learn
   to read their signs
and perceive their sounds
that tend to hide in the wind
Like my mother now, she
   was silent and kept patient
   through every trial
I used to see her walking from place
   to place
revolving her spindle
twisting the wool's whiteness
Threads that in the nighttimes'
   weaving were turned into
   splendid tapestries
Like my brothers and sisters
    -more than once- I tried to learn
     that art, without success
But in my memory I kept
   the content of designs
that spoke of creation
and of the resurgence of the Mapuche
   world
of protective powers, of volcanoes

      flowers and birds
And with my grandfather
    I shared many nights
    in the open air
Long silences, long narratives
     that spoke of the origin
      of our people
of the First Mapuche Spirit
thrown down from the Blue
Of the souls suspended
    in the infinite
    like stars
Taught us of the pathways in the
    sky, its rivers, its signs
Every spring I saw him wearing
    flowers on his ears
and in his jacket lapel
or walking barefoot through
    the morning dew
I also remember him riding a horse
    through immense forests
in the torrential winter rains
He was a firm and lean man

Roaming among brooks, woods
    and clouds, I see the seasons
    passing by:
Moon of cold buds (winter)
Moon of green shoots (spring)
Moon of first fruits
  (the end of spring
    and the beginning of summer)
Moon of plentiful fruits

    (summer)
and Moon of ash-colored buds
    (autumn)

I go out with my mother and father
    to look for medicines
    and mushrooms:
Mint for the stomach
balm for sadness
matico for the liver and for wounds
coralillo for the kidney
    -she would tell me
Dancing, dancing, the medicines
    of the mountains -he would add
making me hold up the plants
    with my hands
That's how I learn the names of flowers
    and herbs
Insects do their work
Nothing is superfluous in this world
Polarity rules the universe
the good does not exist without the bad
The earth does not belong to humans
Mapuche means People of the Land
    -they told me

In autumn the rivers began
    to sparkle
The spirit of the water stirring on the
    stony streambeds
water emerging from the
    Earth's eyes
Every year I ran to the mountains
to witness nature's miraculous

    ceremony
Then winter came to purify
    the Land
for the initiation of new Dreams
    and sown fields
Sometimes the *guairaos* birds
    would fly by announcing
      disease or death
I would suffer thinking one
    of the Elders I loved
would have to part toward the banks
    of the River of Tears
to call out for the rafter of death
and go meet the Ancestors
to feel pleased in the Blue Land
One early morning my brother Carlitos
    departed
It was drizzling, an ash-colored day
I went off and became lost in the forest
    of imagination
      (I am still there)
In autumn the sound of the running streams clasps us in its arms

Today, I tell my sisters Rayen
    and Amerika:
I believe poetry is just
breathing in peace
-as our Jorge Teillier reminds us-
while like the Sky Rhea
I send my sad thoughts wandering over
    every land
And telling Gonza, Gabi, Caui, Malen
    and Beti:
Today I am in the Valley of

the Moon, in Italy
with the poet Gabriele Milli
Today I am in France
with my brother Arauco
Today I am in Sweden
with Juanito Cameron and Lasse
    Söderberg
Today I am in Germany
with my dear Santos Chavez
    an Doris
Today I am in Holland
with Marga with Gonzalo Millan
    and with Jimena, Jan and Aafke
    Juan and Kata

It rains, it drizzles, yellow goes
    the wind in Amsterdam
Canal waters are shinning
 on the old iron lamps
and on the drawbridges
I think I see a blue tulip
a windmill its spinning sails
    taking off
We wish to fly:
Let's go!, may nothing disturb
    my dreams —I tell myself
And I'am carried away on clouds
toward places unknown
    to my heart.

Translated by John Bierhorst y Loreto Pizarro

UNUY QUITA
The Water Sequence (fragment)

Water
and its thirst
are one

......

Unuy Quita

Curving soundulating
magmatic stream

Pacha Pacarina
flashflood sphere

You are one

Waterrrr

Zigzag meander

Spiraling joy

Who filled you with filth?

Chicha gone
around the bend

Playing splashing

Your sack
my span

One thirst!

Shiver you thirst!

Fertile valley

Round water bird

Sacred you cohere

Being yourself!

Flow
forever

Travel
through your blood

Flowing
through yourself

Cup
in the mist

You
yourself

Mist is the semen of the mountains
                where the streams are born
                Mist is the semen of the forest
                where coolness is born

When the mist and the forest are gone,
we will all be gone.
                            Translated by Eliot Weinberger

......

Foggy little fog

Fibrous little fog!
Foggy centipede

Scenting
fertility dancing

We must take care of her flames!
Take care of her smoothness!

How beautiful!
How bountiful!

She said and awoke

Thus she brought all this
back in view

Thus she raised it
shining in its crisscross

Sacred little fire!

Offering of grain

………

The round spring
its own silence
the sylvan key
will end

It will all end!

Where will the fog go?
The life-giving mist?
Where will it go?

Cool, fresh,

The earth's sustenance
The tear-filled branches

Our hearts extinguished
when the fog is gone!

Translated by Suzanne Jill Levine

BOTANICAL GARDEN

A woman feed a dozen of cats
While the twins milk from the wolf.
An old man await for the arrival of winter
Unknown trees but friendly shadows
welcome and I walk around the hills
Following the flight of mask birds
This is the time I need to think, I said to myself
And I sit to receive the warm Fall sunspots
But I cannot think.
I wait for you to pick me up.
Tu
Or Death.

Translated by Mariela Griffor

UNKNOWN
A man I didn't know
appear in all the country's newspapers
He is lying on the streets
His body is perforated:
Now we all know him.

SANTIAGO TANGO
Lack of decency, marginal, preposterous.
Shoeless, armed city.
This one is dying on us
With a stub on the left side
of its veiled face.
poor dam, fur-coated whore
Transpiring pollen
The squalid night double you
Where the pimp sleeps.

THE CAVE
One believes oneself to be the choreography
in the tightrope of life
or the pendulum without towing
but you continue to be the old leak
of a nauseating bedroom
or the fire drills in one night.
We travel in between the legs of a city
You believe to be the rough track

and lose an eye in the wire fence
and why to be believe to be the best
if they trade your vitality in the dessert.

RELEGATION
Yet the words soon will become themselves
José Coronel Urtecho
The thirst was yours
Passing the desert under the skirts
Atacama Ata-cama Ataca -ama des-sierto
Cierto-ama-Ataca-ama amor
Drink the dunes and the sky
disrope yourself of words.

PREMONITION
The crows are coming
black wings
under full sail
from sail to sail
flying ships
deadly polen in the claws scratching:
The sky with black chalk.

Translated by Mariela Griffor

HÉCTOR HERNÁNDEZ MONTECINOS

No!

To make art is to make language, my beloved ones,
Strange, truncated, horrifying, deformed language
Dynamic, flexible and clear as a river.

                Pablo de Rokha............
No to the respectable whores of beauty / No to the distinguished dogs of poetry / We have sung to our generation without achieving to wake them up from fear / We have played to be word spilling shots at ease over the heads of those mouth opened that never imagined an outburst like this for poetry and for what lives of it / We have undressed the dolls with fire and our own voice / We have renounced for them to our logic and our shame / Because when the gods stay silent the atacama deserts of the world blossom inwards into the eyes / We no longer want to be blind / We seek to fight against the despair of time and the demons of power / But only now we have resolved that poetry is a rumour spread by conjurers / And that our fingers are darts / The truth is one of the few lies that hurt in this context / We don't write poetics / We read the joints of life / It was our turn to do the dirty job / To unlock those baby filled sewers because in the beds of my house the sleepers don't cease to grow and they squeeze me and won't let me write and says that we are bad very bad / Honesty is naked / It's nose and ass bleed / We are called to be more than just the first to continue / Our shrouds are seminaries / Nobody wants to touch us / Mi friends don't have more than 22 years / And they know the ambiguity of looks / They know the hallucination of the spheres / They know the exile of the lineage / They know the survivors of 17 years in flames / They know fascism / They know dicta-bland-torship / They know alcohol after sunrise / Boys dancing around the moon / Shed heart / Sacred heart of the rebel /

Hurt and bleeding heart of the homosexuals / Our life is broken / Every genre is a convention we don't need / From one day to another a handful of shinning mixed raced kids appeared from the most inhospitable corners of National Shame / My friends paint the streets with blood semen and tears / My friends make music with the remains of the pretty republic on their knees / My friends occupy houses for culture and are prosecuted / My friends don't spit upwards because they no longer trust in heaven / My friends make videos recording reality / My friends have names of saints but it's just a funny coincidence / My friends make of life a performance with the purpose of not going to hell / My friends are witnesses to sensual revolutions / My friends know the landscapes of Chile because of acid / In the corners of the city we have fought we have gotten drunk we have loved each other / We have been cursed for being less mediocre than our parents / We have multiplied divisions / The past is just a excuse for being a coward / My friends are poor people from the streets in the night / There are also men who suicide among my friends / And the crazed ones are not alone / But we have each other and we have poetry / That's why we celebrate we are together announcing the future of our wishes / The worst that could happen is that we start to gradually shut up / To fall get tangled in the same gallop / Men-women-horses / We are living the mourning of our times / No to the respectable whores of beauty / No to the distinguished dogs of poetry.

Translated by Rodrigo Olavarría

OLIVER WELDEN

THE PARTY

I hear dying. My face is disintegrating.
I go on growing old in the night with a hand
in my mouth. My vomit trails off the bed
paddling down. I'm naked waiting. I hear dying.
The room nailed in the silence blinks. I hide myself.
But how poorly you conceal yourself you son of a bitch.

Translation by Dave Oliphant

BINNACLE

I love the apple core you ate down to,
stuck in the ashtray, with my cigarette buts,
its seeds and stem left behind
simply so I may look at them
and remember that where you are isn't far,
though I'll never know the way.

Translation by Dave Oliphant

FLUCTUATIONS

It may be that too much time has passed,
more than enough, but I figure it's necessary
to keep waitingfor the tide to go out
in order to tie my bodyto the half-submerged rock,

to close my eyes and open my mouth
and wait, once more, for the surf to rise.

Translation by Dave Oliphant

I WOULD HAVE LIKED TO HAVE STAYED HERE

A wedding song composed of unmoving air,
of dry earth, for giving you a new dimension
of love, I deposit in a roll of paper
through the keyhole of the door of your home, as
I grow old returning to my dust and to my night.

Translation by Dave Oliphant

TIERRA DEL FUEGO

*for quite some time nobody reads in this city books burned in fantastic
pyres and when confronted with the written word the citizens lowered
their eyes filled with confusion and shame*
Omar Lara

The next day Wednesday September 12th 1973
we burned books in a large hole dug with a shovel
and at dawn of Thursday 13th and at noon of Friday 14th
with care in the back yard so as not to raise a column of smoke
in Spring that could be seen from the hills: soldiers/binoculars
with care that the sun had already risen so the fire would go unseen
with care that the sun had already set
so the fire of the books we burned would go unseen

English version by the author

PASSER-BY

from his eyes he was crying deeply and turning his head he looked at his people
El Cid

You never let go of your bag in exile
not a coffer of sand perhaps what rags memor
ies old pieces of junk from another continent lati
tude dawn and sunset from south to north
aurora australis of your dark and distant country
the image of a cordillera intac
t because they can't move it slide it
push it back like a latin american prepuce.
And now that it is cold again but it has al
ways been cold your coffer trunk suitcase ba
g you drag rumpled through borders ol
der faded but yours Chilean
of sixty something years old again with pass
port stamped sealed renewed sig
ned by the consul Dog on the loose by force
of military boot you go To the immi
gration officer you hand a little piece of paper that says
only: such is life and then comes someone
and jerks it: life is a whore and then you die

English version by the author

I GLEAN
To Carlos Cortínez

The set on edge praise of the mirror
Envia birds to the electrica chair.
We have come back when our armor of
Embers played cards to losing it again
Inmobile near the summer.

DESPERATE WITH YOU
To Diana Camacho B

If, this night the eternity riks in our
Blood and before that I the deciphering
Covers your body.
Dou you remember that in spite of only
Fixing the ardor of a chest to him
The forest was ours?
Since I desperte with you the waters turned
Us indelible and the days and the nights
They are kept as in complete falls.

JULIO PIÑONES

FINANCIAL REALM

Some uncertainties move away.
Others come by.
The subterfuge is raised up as a method
to avoid problems.
 Disturbances occurred the same.
They may be fruit of comparisons
if the levels of living are compared
the possibilities are more or least.
Comparisons are odious it is known.
Official statistics can't stand
the least analysis. The craft of the ophidian
consists of unfolding a fan of hypothesis
so that its master deceives the unfortunate.
Bankers do not forgive their indebted.
Bank robbers have a hundred years of forgiveness.
The ones everyone knows jump on the run to the last carriage.
The same ones smell out to achieve Power.
Work lowers its price at the market.
Salesmen must attain their goals without scrupulous
Folders look full
of frauds.

THE SOBER UNFORTUNATE

They are characterized for keeping their dignity.
Their dignity lies in their principles.
Their principles are incompatible
to walk arrogantly provoking along the streets
In front of any mess
their principles compel them to maintain tidiness.

They have turned misfortune into their discipline.
Prisons into their lecture rooms of temperance.
They receive with patience the mistreatment of the world.
They expel from themselves every inch of resentment.
The know that life has many turns.
That's why they watch how the new hand of poker comes.

HEAVEN I'M IN HEAVEN

Today they dance in no *heaven*.
In other époques they blow out dance floors.
With elegance, he took her firmly by the waist
They spin in the dancing rink without thinking in the future.

The rhythms of the orchestras
Produced triumphant couplings.
They would have wished to be kept floating in the air.
Today they dance in no heaven.

VERÓNICA JIMÉNEZ

MARINA ARRIVES WITH THE RAIN

Taken in with you like a dream
I neither forget nor remember.
Sing the winter and I part from the others
words newly born:
those that we leave under the arc of pain
as we pass by trembling,
those that I wove into your wings
so your flight commands
the surrounding clay
the chaotic solitude which forsakes.

The night is a lamp and pours out
in a blast the oil of goodbyes.
In my pluvial dream the shadows cry out.
The relentless markers of the future
come and go like extras,
like tepid storms on a sea lacking salt
       pyramids of weeping.
I neither remember nor forget.
I thread the convulsive needle
that rips me from your body
to gather you up the polished
superhumanness of the day.

       Wait for us on your border
       Rain that is here in the rain
       Synthesis of water
       See us as we are
       See how we fall in this

        A permanent prisoner of time
            This is life.

You grow up in comfort, you believe so you can see the sun
it soon surprises you – a blast of air
and this emptiness
furnished with instruments of torture.
Your fine blood issues forth in a circle
to enter another –
an abyss intense and throbbing.
You advance while time backs away
and the beginning of innocence retires from the groove.

        Bird of fire, free us
        From your wild roots.

Your hands cling to a corner of the cloth
To a point of destiny.

The rain crosses the backwater of my dream,
drags along the current of other days and sings
bleaching the cesspool of the afternoon.

I sleep with a girl wrapped in air.

The rain sings into the heart of a seed
scratches up the earth and pulls up roots: words
newly come.
Like in a cosmic dance
next comes the sun bearing miniature suns,
yours are sons of mine
together we play with these little ones

that will illuminate you,
Friend of the clouds
Daughter of the rain.

Daughter of the rain,
chain of beautiful looks, linger
under my eyes, search the fire
your visions as you call them
fill my dreams, a sun
of gilded roots
rides on your back,
my hand flows over your body
wants to fill you,
child who comes from what is full
to that which fails you.

Before you, came my mother to spread herself on my side
her body lit a flame in my blood
a bonfire of premonitions
my mother fashioned herself in me
I was her island
through me, arrived a latent sea
but my feet burned.
I was filled with my mother,
duplicating her stride
dragging myself like a shadow
by her shores.
She extended her gaze over me
and in a vision of ardent fire
you reclined as well, reunited
sap of our glances.
I burned over the face of my mother

dreaming myself a girl who wove souls,
outlining paths over the water
to arrive at you, root hastened,
simultaneous deep journey
in my unoccupied body.
Now my mother empties herself newly in me
I am her forge
I embrace slow wards that unite
in a dream that burns.

I sleep with a girl wrapped in air.

This
is not a poem. You move in a dream
of tossed waters,
the lamp tumbles anew
and the fire runs over,
your eyes so able to look inside me
ignite distant bonfires.

The fire defines contours of water
drops disperse in collections
of columns that open like arms
in an ornamental sky, empty.

I search for hexagonal words,
a prism that opens across the page, faults
those who write stark measures.

Your hands lazy over my chest
open and close my books.
The guard of our dream is a sleepy one.

SINS

All the demons
came to us.
One by one we were falling.
Fate was already known,
God has abandoned us.

DIZZINESS

I did n`t go beyond the cliffs.
I just knew your hands so closely
and the softness of your look.
I've always been afraid of heights.

SUNDAY'S VISITOR

I have always been dead.
You have come to wake me up here,
deep inside the earth.

PROVISIONAL INVENTORY

The old clay is cursed to itself,
humid in the middle of the summer,
while our shoes
demand their right to be on the table.

Probably would be this the ocassion
to regret not to have been
a little more heroic
at the moment of to set sail.

Not they to have broken some spears
-at least one-
to have something more than say
in the late of these harbors.

The inventory of hugs
does more inhospitable the place.
Someone blows on the table,
as frightening a curse.

ORACLE OF DELPHI.

Ingenuous rite
to be looked,
        regardless.

With the torn mirrors,
the fingers condemned to the ink,
to the tobacco,
it seems that yet it is time
to conquer the wisdom of the silence,
granted as example

slightly minuscule,
if we think that the Oracle of Delphi has closed,
finally, for lack of clients.

The memory offers winks
that try to warm these corners.

Nevertheless,
here,
    only it is cold.

SERGIO ARRAU CASTILLO

SOUTHERN ONE

Beach flare and trembling sand
beating fruition of tense meat
entity shatters into a thousand pieces
spilling into sudden warmth.

I even forgot who the hell I was
permanent high tension
everything else wasn't worth a damn
just being with you once more and that's it.

How many rooms furtively gone around
seeing everywhere closed doors
hearth as timbales in F major
and the great consolation of fresh sheets.

It was heaven and hell at every hour
with sweetness and sour reproaches
permanent jealous blackmailing
for months and years which flew as water.

And setting off and coming back and new energies
roofs and apartments again
leaving the key on the little table
a century in a minute passed by.

Black and white at the same time
unattached passion hate returned
slid over glass cones
submerging nerves and tendons.

With exquisite smoothness you filled
up the clown with breasts and knees
even if I were a thousand leagues away
just by thinking of you the radium burned.

It was like dying from a single hit
having you again between my arms
exploring your geography discovering
new and unending gold veins.

And suddenly hate sparkled again
I would have stomped your head
swearing never to return I was fleeing then
to that rampant schizophrenia.

But then I kept finding you
walking with your biblical grace
a single look was enough to break
the Western Wall into four thousand pieces.

We gave ourselves everything and we gave ourselves nothing
the desert wind blows above the dunes
erasing clues of a startled flower
and the corpse of the bird who died of infinity.

But I can't erase pale scars
which often fester and bleed
impossible of covering up with T-shirts
with the hope of an I need you
that would make me fly to find
I don't know what of immortal
in your somber eyes.

UNDERLIES

Underlies an unwritten history
Against the official one in the surface
Underlies the everlasting warrior
Against slavery,
Softened
Underlies the glory of the mosses
Against the cement jungle
Underlies the mythological female
Against the object woman
Underlies the art of the wizard against the trendy artist
Underlies
The free man in the paths of the world
Underlies the honour under the contracts,
The bills
Wandering from stars and parallel colors
Underlies the ivy
Underlies the love
Underlies an alphaoceanic rasping breath
Under the dead of the forgetfulness
Underlies the night
Underlie I
Underlie the genes of the cosmos
Under the appetite of the earth
(Underlies the wisdom of the intelligence)
Underlies the florid promise of the Sacred Word
Underlies the sea
Underlies the man
Underlies the light
Underlies the life in the south of the time.

IT IS NECESSARY TO CONTINUE THE AMAZEMENT
FIRST VOICE (FRAGMENTS)

What territorial hand will set
on the dust of days
Sundays
in spite of the utopias that escape us?
As if we were
unraveling dusty roads
built by the hands of rustic workmen
beyond laughter and the clumsiness of the eyes
angels that laugh go by
the abundance of neighborhood markets

And you come
with long steps along the side walks
among balloons in the air
with all the ideals about to burst.

Here
in this land of honey
where your mother defoliated her life
and used to extend her hand between oceans
there remain voices without protection that ask
about the great things learned
about the simplicity of names
Here they wait
to the North and to the South
to the East and to the West
the necessary days that we had
in the recesses of the doors.

Here
to the South West of the city
where poetry hangs in the late afternoons
by the four sides
and where in long braids
you used to play along ancient corridors
among paintings and portraits of grandmother
that phrase that triggers your heart at dawn
still resounds through the large windows
that face the garden
"When are you coming by the house, daughter?"
…as if it were easy to meet
the afternoons multiplying the rainbow.

Here from tables of towns
from coves and terminals of buses
from mines and factories
from orchards and the syndicate
From the North to the South
we build murals
on which we write our names

It was the time of the inevitable gesture
illuminated by open wounds
while our heart stooped
and the sun scattered over our heads

How young and beautiful we were in the native land one day!

Here the North awaits you
with voices and yards
of nameless cities

With its forgotten saltpeter mines
surviving
as one coming back
from painful events

With skies and tracks
with suits and hats of ancestral spaceships
planting the deserts
so that we don't have to invent for ourselves birds
and flowers.

Here the permanence of the South greets you
reclaiming with its rains and volcanoes;
offering its millenarian forests
where the "copihue" in love braids itself
of oaks carob and cinnamon trees

Where we can take down the stars
in some way
and support the birds that travel
where only they know.

Here
we also knew about interior exiles
In this great house that awaits you
we repressed the sound
of our own breathing
avoiding the night to fall
on our heritage
We seemed angels
with broom and white apron
on ruined corridors
invaded with cherry trees.

Here
at the bottom of ourselves
There are raised names, which in us live!

CARMEN RODRÍGUEZ

?

What did my brother feel that deep hollow August night
hospital bed
needles tubes probes   invasion of orifices

What did my brother feel
majestic grey whale
aground   solitary beach
warm lethal sand
and the pulse of the sea   so close   unreachable

Did he see the sun   hear the ocean burst
                  in his memory
listen to the train whistle
recite Antilhue Pishuinco Huellelhue
the way we did so many times   as children
      on the way to Valdivia
feet hanging from the third class bench
floor carpeted with baskets and bundles
trees river cows rain
      travelling back
      through the window
steam engine soot blackening our eyelids

What fires did you rekindle that last August night, Nelson
      a blow from your torturer
      a lover's stroke
      the whine of a door opening
      Ceci's laughter bouncing into the room
Did you write the last line to that poem

abandoned on your working table

Did you look for the shoes
that slipped off your feet   at your door
as they got you in the ambulance

I have them, *gordo*
put them away   brown paper bag
front hall closet   my place

What am I going to do with your shoes
now that you have gone

AMBUSH IN CHINATOWN

Naked ducks hang   golden
tongues poke out of bivalves
surprised   silence

blue day
Strathcona homes soaked in sun
windows dressed as brides

centenary bricks   neighbourhood school

from the rustle in the school yard
covered with autumn
jumps   sudden ambush

notebooks ribbons smocks boots
broken images   gallop
glisten and hide again

in the crevices of my body

SUBJECT

I've created a world for myself
some old clothes
a few books
the table
music
a place occupied by order
harmony
the play of colours and textures
and dry
white
wine
moving this bitter hand
before the authorized invasion of
man
children
a job
kitchen
necessary enemies
of this part of me
that rejoices in
solitary
cellular
space
of my own making
here
inside
this night outside
inside of me
this I

GABRIEL LARENAS

TO INGRID BETANCOURT

Ingrid,
what is there to see?
could I walk into your mind
in greed
to join your sounds,
the prision, the jungle
and then come back to my house?

Ingrid,
I know your demons,
I've smelt their guns;
in greed
in pain, I'm bound
to your wordless reflections,
your unspeaking memory,
the unpronounced body
I look for in my own land.

I know,
the head, it falls
before the rain,
forgetting the sense of brains,
the head
falls down.
I've noticed
in each and every trail,
and when it rains
what is there to see?
In trees and weapons

what is there to hear?
Besides
war and hunger.

Ingrid,
we all eat silence
in greed,
we vex our souls.
Be patient,
so I can be courageous,
Be senseless,
so I can write about this land,
so I can change all deviations,
transgress our politicians,
or at least let no one to be proud.

POEMS AND WORDS
THE WORD

What is the word?
An incomplete whiff
The synthesis of a glance
An attempt, brief, little is the word
The way between the reality and our mirror
All-consuming of colors and memories
That they deform all it .
Principio del formulario
But, even so, rare
And everything what is
The word is
The best option to portray
The forgetfulness .

YOUR WORDS, YOUR LIFE

That they are not the words
hindrance in your heroic attempt
still it is possible, see and lives
it raises your tired eyebrows
and it leaves enters the ocean
with its colors and rumors
about your you will think, in your corners
in your unfinished desires.

That they are not the words, yours
ghosts of so many fears
hidden in several bends
of your journeyed footpath.

Your way comes fast, thirsty
and one appears dusty in the summer
emphasizing the impatient life
they continue the shouts in your biography
still they are words that to write.

Perhaps they are these, mine
A backwater of love, these words
A song to your beautiful smile

CEREMONIAL REMAINS

First
it was a tree
then
it cast itself
into stone
eternal witness
of a wounded
landscape
grew
surrounded
by cities
that the time
has reduced
to a portion
of dust
and a handful
of ashes
that the wind
spreads
and the rain
erases

BACK IN LA PINTANA

After too long
an absence

Eternally tired

In the darkness
of the memories
and remote places
Here I am again
in the shantytown
of La Pintana
listening
to the sound
of the rain
falling
on a rusty
tin roof

VÍCTOR SEPÚLVEDA CARRASCO

TO PERSIST

All
the doors
have been closed
to me,
one by one.
I stubbornly built
my expectations,
nevertheless.
Then
I got myself
into an envelope.
And
someone
(perhaps, a postman)
helped me
to penetrate
by cracks
between
the doors
and soil
of shacks and mansions.

SHE-WOLF

As still as still lying on my bed
weary from the unceasing tedium
of endless chores
I try to calm myself, my body,
bit by bit
until it breathes but
the stillness of the night.

Outside the thickening fog
its ethereal particles
moving ever in a restless dance
seeking a home they will never know.

I see alone the bloody eye
of the moon above
spying on me
behind the hurrying clouds
from distant hidden corners of the sky.

I hear the call of the wetlands
louder and louder
entering my ears, invading my heart,
making me leap out
from that senseless body
lying on my bed.

I burst out felling
the heavy-knockered door
feeling the way with my claws

eyes ablaze in the night
mane bristling and
nakedness covered by dusky pelts
that I have never worn but
I know are mine.

I feel my nostrils twitching
as they scoop the night air in
Eyes half closed I breathe deep
and deep again
till I shed the last of the foolish humanity
of that faraway body lying on my bed.

I track the sickly sweet scent of the forest
the smell of earth and the trees
and plunge into the undergrowth
damp with the night and the fog
where other she-wolves wait.

Some howl in unison their pain or their rage,
some sit licking their private wounds
alone in the shelter of the wood
Still others go deeper in
up and down by unknown paths
to the place of meeting
where like wild horses they copulate,
their bodies wrapped in the fog
that begins to rise
slow, thick and warm
from the very vortex where life begins.

I am the mountain peering down from my summit
My eyes intently scan
the slippery shining breasts of rock

to the thin line of brush at the edge and
then search into the density of the forest
whence hazy and hot
the steam emerges from the boiling depths
where, manes flowing free,
the horses mate then part
and gallop off taking their separate ways.

The light of dawn is near
and so the need to return
to that body lying on my bed

When the last trace of fog has gone
the she-wolf rises, once again the woman
to wrangle with her man
to prepare the meal
to take the children off to school...

FIRST MEETING

I declare myself the alma mater
of this wandering days
and I run away to the white
calendar face
Nobody's earth crackles
fertile and grieving
the moon breaks crimson
while you cover
your imaginary sex
I see you satanic
and constellated
under the flowery notro
I watch you, I smell you
I wait for you
I set you free to the wind
my carnivorous hair
and a roar of pink clouds
finally pronounces
the name of all days…

HAUGHTY

I am going straight to you
and I offer myself
like an empty fountain
I go finding you
in the deserted way
behind every step
far from your closed window
and I ride the dawn
over this hills
blues of misery
Only for you to understand
that this piled-up bones creaking
is the answer to the daring
of repeating –to myself-
and a million times
the sixth Commandment

FLASHBACK

After the most sublime time
has passed
she slides
along the bright corridor
of the old house
at the end, behind the crystals
the illuminated pear-tree and fruit-trees
Then I, hidden and minute
wearing me feet
in the wide heels space
owners of other histories.

DAVID ÁLVAR DE CASTRO

THE POOR MAN'S LOT

Grudgingly, in the cold,
I let go of my pillow and
Leave my bed startled by the sound
Of the alarm clock
Than never ends.

I open the window,
Letting the early morning air
Breathe life into my room.

I can see the new sun, rising
Over the snow-covered peaks
Of the Andes.

The sun's rays bring in
The crystalline glow
Of a blossoming light,
Radiating gloriously into my home —
Filtering through
Even the small cracks
In the walls of my rustic shack. —
It is new hope for the day that begins.

I make myself a tea
And warm up a piece of bread
In the ashes of the brazier
Still glowing
Overnight.

I leave early in the morning, reluctantly.
My hands sunk deep into my pockets.
Only the fresh autumn breeze
Pushes me forwards towards my workplace.

The chilly wind also blows the last remaining
Leaves off the great trees
Along Forester Park.

Unexpectedly,
I cough up my cold, harshly. —
It's a bitch, the poor man's lot! I grumble.
Everyday, sunny or cold, hungry or tired
You've got to work: scraping your hands
Or breaking your back and
All that,
For what?

Only so one may do it
All over again the following day, and
Again the day after that. —
There is no future for the poor!

I can see the gypsies
By The Arts Palace.
Round layered skirts down to their ankles.

"Give me your palm!" they demand.
They want to read your fortune.

I shoo them away as if they were flies.
What fortune may I have that
I have yet to be told?
For me,

It's always been —
Misery!

JUAN GARRIDO-SALGADO

SONNET (WRITERS' WEEK IN ADELAIDE, 2006)

I am sitting in different shadows.
Chairs are the roots of trees,
the white tents a nest of words and creation.
I am listening to the sound and face of vowels.
Names and authors are beings of the image world.
Stories of lands, struggles, deaths,
beauty and ugliness an equal part of the journey.
Foreign sounds are rare birds under native trees.
A kookaburra sings to the wind and the heat of the evening.
Yahia Al-Samawy reads his poem in Arabic:
Leave my country.
The helmet of occupiers can never be a pigeon's nest
I am listening to the rhythm of hearts next to a tree.
I am listening to Robert Fisk's flesh,
wounded lines,
Baghdad and Gaza his home,
ancient cities without rivers,
only dried dreams of the oppressors.

SEPTEMBER 11, 1973
In memory of all those who struggled for freedom and justice in Chile against the fascism of Pinochet
Santiago, September 11, 1973,

What a dark spring
Of terror, flames and fumes.
Two jets
Flew like the evil wings of death,

Made in the USA.

Soldiers in the streets formed part
Of the scaffold of violence from the sky,
Rivers of blood ran through our mouths,

Made in the USA.

Dark flowers grew on the table
Beneath our nocturnal silence.
The singer was tortured.
Socialism was a harvest burning in the field,

Made in the USA.

Victor Jara* sung his *último poema***
In the stadium of pain and howls of horror.
An hour before he was shot
His guitar was burnt.
Wounded doves, wounded words:
Embers in an eternal song,

Made in the USA.

September 11, 1973,
From the North, Kissinger awakes
To converse with Nixon in the White House;
The two of them were smiling that morning in September,

Made in the USA.
* *Victor Jara is a political folk singer*
**last poem

ALEJANDRO MUJICA-OLEA

THE WILLOW

Willow of emerald
with your Beatles wig.
The wind balancing your bushy hair
with a Latin rhythm that rises
and falls, recedes and advances.
This is the cha, cha, cha,
of the afternoon
with its magic
flashes of green
and yellow sparkles.

The rest of the grove
is immobile
only the willow plays
like the children
of the neighborhood.

It is an afternoon
fragrant, typical of summer
in Queensborough
on this July first,
Day of Canada.

Translated by Ariadne Sawyer

RAMÓN SEPÚLVEDA

YOU LEFT ME FOR A VEGETARIAN MAN.

no one called me.
there was no letter, no email.
it was you who said it.

you had met him art the Green Door restaurant
he had long hair and magnetic bracelets
forty'sh and unemployed.

but he was your soul mate
your mirror
your spiritual mentor.
he would cook tahini and quinoa
and would only drink organic wine.

and I, instead of questioning the wine,
asked, "how would you know about his kitchen?
his table?
his bedroom?

you took the time to explain
to clarify my doubts,
and finally,
to confirm my fears,
"but let's make peace," you said
and invited me for dinner.

"you, him and I for dinner?
what the hell have you taken me for?
the three of us at the same table

asparagus, spinach and oregano omelettes
balaclava for dessert.

no thanks,
save me from carrots
eggplants or zucchini
save me the indigestion that I see coming.

no thank you.

LUIS CORREA-DÍAZ

LAMB OF GOD

> *Little Lamb, who made thee?*
> *Dost thou know who made thee?*
> *William Blake*

This time I fucked up
all at once I am playing the game
that most pleases Our Lady of Solitude the bitch
and in her own house to make matters worse I believe all she says
is happening out there it is the only thing that makes her
to speak in tongues throwing coal into my fear nibbling my
        brains abusing
some poor childish devil buzzing like a queen
around the ashes of memory installing herself between an eyebrow
        and another
sticking her filthy hand in the soup of the mirror chasing with
        her bulging voice
dreams in the garden of earthly delights opening an eye
with the cigarette to every flower covering the sun amidst the tiring
gasp
that creeps through her by a pure silence calling its belfry
for curfew and smashing one's face with a masterful blow
only to then unforgivable act force him to starve
ordering him to enter alone into darkness
single bed where she will arrive later inebriated
of herself but cold as a tombstone that blind d/fate
with/of a common place where those who delay their suicide spawn
        and argue with little angels
in platonic chats meanwhile they punish themselves from their back
fetal indulgence at any price because she pays in gold the idolatry

drops of blood semen tears and the sweet slobber
of the smile the capital puddle in which the lamb awakens
and may the reader end in allegory if so desired

Translated by Frances Franch

DIGNITAS TERRAE AND SOME OTHER ECO-CANTOS

I just came back from the play –I told you that was
going to be my evening, in the company of some
beloved friends, entertained by Boal's hilarious
counter-imperialist fantasy, translated and adapted
by RM-, and now sitting on the porch with a half-full
or a half-empty glass of wine in my hand, I don't do
anything but think about the eclipse we had
last night, pondering how life brings me all I
long for in such a conflicting way –'once again,'
I caught my heart murmuring while hesitating whether
to send this e-mail or not… Anyhow, fully supplied
with cigarettes I let myself enter into the ghostly rigor
of this night until it ends, already waiting for…, for what?
what else! –next Thurs lunch with you, and of course
the following one, when we'll resume (sitting across from
each other, in your sisterly eyes all the restaurant needs
from Brother Sun) our conversation on how we are to preserve
-today's praising, before it's too late-

INSOMNIA

It would be impossible to get rid of
these apathetic eyes: staring into the darkness of a sleeping room,
watching the time-drop slowly form and fatten,
slipping off into an abyss of blurry memories;
To forget these heavy eyelids,
curtains for this morbid theater of repetition.

Silence could never exist in this statue world
of blank walls and turning pillows.
Every creak gets through: the nibble of a finger
scratching against the white sheets, the wheezing of the red digital clock
gleaming into the darkness of the room,
Your breath…

I turn and for one moment it has all disappeared
I try to start again; the sheets are cold and my thoughts have been erased.
But it is impossible to escape that sound, that thought;
The red reminder that the minute drops have formed again and again.
That hours have gone by and I have not been able to get rid of
These apathetic eyes, the blank white wall
My broken record thoughts.

THE TUBE

I miss my metro stops daydreaming
in the tube of the subconscious
and wake up waiting
on the automatic steps which
tick to the time on my mobile.
Love rushes by in pics of the past;
black against the backs of their reflections.
I sink into the temporary scenes
like dreams; People pass, sit down and laugh.
Men stare with eager eyes, but mine
are lost in space- in the spaces
between them.

I go over the lesson in my head
like a dead person, mind subdued;
nothing new in this daily bread.
His love was but a window fleeting past,
not made to last too many stops.
But my dreams are like the wind,
they howl into each hollow corner.

It's just a dream now don't
mistake it for your life!
I say to my best friend that
girl who stands at the end
of the metro lost
in her own thoughts- daydreaming.

But she looks down into the gap
we have to mind on the underground:
It's deep and dark and horrifying.

PAULINA RAMIRÉZ

IMPACT OF SEPTEMBER

Gathering crumbs in search of me
I stumbled on the condor's humble prey.
Tumbling forward in my American way
I was assailed by the silence as I blundered

to a carcass of a man
who, like a huemul, failed
to dissimulate or abate,
a trembling memory in his eyes.

"What was it like?"
I brazened, then explained,
"I was raised in a free land whose scholar
unleashed Chicago winds to wreak
a liberal sovereign dollar.

I read of the success of ideal economics
and transparent business practices
among corrupt republics."

Like a wounded deer
his eyes kicked wildly through the air until,
resigned to run no more, he rested,
quelled his fears and spilled
his testament,

"If you want to know what life was like
before the coin's ore was blown to bits
on the eleventh of September prior

to the one that you remember,
go to where I go now to forget.

It takes two days to get there, where
no rivers hide the wide open secrets of the general.
The island's veins run pure and cold
to soothe the seething blood of molten rock
holding humble homes on poles
waltzing with Pacific waves.

A dolphin escort leads you homeward
toward mythical bards forsaken by the fray."
A rack soon swept his harbor
from the main his affliction returned to grieve
again, his eyes resumed their doleful mien
coerced by this woeful history.

"Before you drink elephant grapes, think—
a soldier in a teacher's place, a rollcall from the oasis to the stadium, missing themistopoloi replaced by
retrospective regimental razors.

Picture dinner blankets made of iron
when one wins with an other's disappearance".
Then the deer-man's voice and eyes expired.

And as I hear the news today of laws that change
under pretext, I sit at my desk afraid
to test inquiries of banned works I cannot see
lest the address I type deem me a person
of interest to the guards of the "free"
who are allowed to keep me, detained, chained,
unsustained in far off secret camps,

I think of him, defeated, afraid to speak
his mind, the price he paid for economic strength,
and realize the full potential of November against
the unchecked impact of September.

A WALTZ FOR MYSELF

one two three one two three
a waltz and a poem
for the evening and I
a sad yellow dream
defeats all the leaves
that cry for their fall
far so far from the sea
one two three one two three
a waltz and a poem
for the evening and I
the whiskey and the smoke
the silence is here
my house is now neat
and is ready to dance
the tortoise in the clock
in the garret the boy
my cat in the roof
my mother outside
and the moon and the pine
one two three one two three
a waltz and a poem
for the evening and I
round after round
the whiskey and the smoke
round after round
my things are now far
a flower is sad
a memory is weak
and in silence a mirror

distills all its salt
round after round
the rain and the leaves
round after round
the hours are gone
and here is Death
sprinkling my books
with a pen of the night
and a verse and an end.

NIEVES FUENZALIDA

THREE OF US REMAIN (fragment)

At eight o'clock the same morning
We heard a man's voice
Saying,
"Rosa…
Nieves…
to the fence

The "guardian" took us to the fence,

"Rosa…
Nieves…
fix your things…
you will be transferred in
five minutes to the
National Correctional Jail
For Women".

Rosa and I look at each other.
We embrace.
I had diarrhea.
I have to confront once more my fear
I will begin another phase
in this nightmare
that now nears
one year.
We fixed our suitcases quickly,
that is to say,
"our cardboard boxes."
We had accumulated a few

in this nightmare.
We left through that door,
all the women that remained
in the "mansion"
came close to the barber wire,
they began to sing
"ode to joy"
and
their hands waver good by.
We walked slowly,
looking behind us.
The "guardian" woman who escorts us
looks at us
and says,

"Be happy…it is freedom!

We released the "boxes"
we embraced.
The women at the barbed wire
understood.

THE DEAD

I can see
my own death
in the subtle reflection
of old clocks;
just one
among so many deaths which are
inconsequential.

An uneasy
sensation of collapsing,
bit by bit,
without reprieve
or meaning.

White bread, familiar songs, poems and roses
do not make any sense;
nor the whispering wind
among the trees,
nor the persistence of so many memories.

There is a painful sadness,
at the end of the journey:
the frustration, the anguish
and the loneliness
of the useless pursuit
of wilted dreams.

There will be new springs
with blooming orchards,

but these won't be by then my own sweet flowers.
There will be deep blue skies
with clouds
and rainbows,
but my clouds and my skies
will be no more.

Others
will come with hopes, and dreams, and feelings.
In a cycle as old and inescapable
as time itself,
they will sow their own luminous seed
of arcane meaning.

Then,
they too will pass on,
inconsequentially,
like the falling snowflakes
in the foreboding
emptiness of winter.

REQUIEM FOR A GENTLE WARRIOR

When you fell to the ground
time stood
still;
and the arrow
was frozen
in the air.

Gentle warrior,
of many a worthy struggle,

time has come
to an end.

The wind
is just a breeze
caressing the green needles
of the pines,
high above
the disappearing patches
of old snow.

Perhaps you took a glance,
one final glance
of sky,
and distant clouds
and sunlight.

No thunder:
only whispers of life
and spring returning,
as you lay
in the meadow
of eternity.

TERESA GONZÁLEZ-LEE

TIJUANA   YOUR 'GREEN" HEART

Tijuana   a cosmos in the US/Mexican border
a segment in an itinerary between two delirious worlds
mirroring   opposing each other.

Tijuana   your painterly image
is that of a two headed horse
one looking South   one looking North.

Tijuana   you're the installation
set up by an artist   showing us how history
needs to shed light on the present to creatively free your future.

Tourist   my friend if you visit T.J   reach out to the residential
hills
step away from the feverish   beehive of Downtown.

Climb up   and firmly set foot
in one of those recycled neighborhoods
that bravely   hang down from the cliffs.

You'll be amazed   by the Mayan style
in the geometry of lines   by the ingenuity displayed
at recycling first world urban waste

You'll be surprised
by the city's kaleidoscope of colors and lights,
by the superb luster of 'green'   in its ecological heart

Student   my friend
admire how countless   ceramic art works
sit tall   impressive   behind windows
while freshly picked flowers   erected   alive
 look outside   defying a plastic urban design.

Discover my friend   Tijuana's artistic side
its unique environmentalism
a 'green' heart where two opposing countries abide
A beauty found in a practical aesthetics
A creative eye for what's humanely profound.

THE PEOPLE

When the generals
offered peace
to the people
if they surrendered,
the people responded:
we will give
you peace
once you lay down your arms!

VÍCTOR OLIVARES ANDREANI

WHILE...

While the winter sheathes its sword
and accepts in its hands the sky's gold,
the air allows drops to fall dry
from it's white mask
that can no longer retain,
and makes ready the green spirits
to be reborn with their gypsy wings
exhumed from the humidity,
re-creating the vivid aromas
until they can hide the years we plow
through time and its clocks.
And baptized by the Holy Mother
we feel sublime and younger
wrapped in a secret gleam
being claimed by our serene eyes.

While winter burns in a photograph
and will be unable to see what the harvest will bring forth,
other angels will reclaim the light
of all our intrinsic veins,
and they will give it to the fields of wind,
so the road opens up at our feet
guided by the echoes of the stars
that leave secret signs
of an old city that happily sprouts
with its new body of a beloved child.
And as we are all filled with music, all inebriated,
Altogether going to the same destination,

I will emerge lifting the flame that tells the soul
how much I love you.

Translated by María Luisa Martînez

ODYSSEY

All roads
take you back to Ithaca
where a woman
awaits for you
But the singing
of mermaids
will have already
made you insane

                      and the young maids
                      will have seduced you
                      and the Cyclops
will have crushed your bones
defeated your bow
bended your arrows

You will return
in spite of the fact
that love does not persist
only its memory
                      –Penelope
                      Why have you waited
for me?

LOT'S WOMAN

        Wise men
        once more
        recommend
        to walk
        But I will look back
        even if I turn
        into salt

ERIK MARTÍNEZ

EVENING DREAMS UPON THE HUMID EARTH

Evening dreams that were other dreams forgotten
no: we did not come walking along the paths of evening
we did not drink the leaf that moistened the dying sun
but constrained and gasping amid the foliage quivering agitated
Ah! If all the heat's blood
if all the plant vapours
lingered in the darkening evening
if all the cries of the birds of luxuriant plumage

I will go rolling a hoop
I will rise naked to bathe in the air of the heights
(there will be a lethargic tree
complaining weakly)
I will cross an immense plain
when the warm weather comes

The green-winged owl
the owl who watched her kinfolk and urinated as she could
through the hole in a certain paper
the nocturnal owl, pestilent lady of round trees
traced her flight like a lost line
a spiral and burrowed into the earth in penance
(oh suffering head of sadness dry your tears
or I will bury the black knife in my belly).

Every living thing made manifest its exuberance
the tree rocked its crown
its leaf swelled green in the green luminosity of the night
and there was a profusion of plant life

the tree grew in the aroma of its boughs
and every living aroma throbbed in the fever of the night.
The spirit of the forest made this bountiful sea to sway
made this tide rise up to the heated face of the skies
and every living thing made manifest its exuberance.

But the inhabitant dreamed upon the humid earth
that his body was fading in the foliage
that his eyes (the last shining sign of his body)
were sinking into a shadow denser than the night
he dreamed that the green leaf's heat was taking over the throb
of his heart (made of a weak material, made
of a red weave of -tissues).
And the arms of the forest reached out to embrace him
and everything happened far away, in the shadows
amid the magnificent living exuberance of the wood
amid those magnificent aromas of the night.

The nocturnal owl, pestilent lady of round trees
traced her flight like a lost line
a spiral and burrowed into the earth in penance

Translated by Christina Shantz

HIGHWAVE

When the world is a curved horizon
immense
like the sandbars on the moon
deep at sea
I am born of the birds a still point
a board
suspended over
the sea
a turn
a flight of words
between foam sharks
a huge wave
of
the
other
rising with the tide of the indistinct
an empty name
a tempest
the son of nothingness

Santiago de Chile, 2005. Translated by María Teresa Borys

THREE WOMEN, A PIANO, A CAT AND A TEMPEST
To Alexandra Keim

It is difficult to be a bird
and to fly against the tempest over
the scar of the Earth

better to be like a cat
always attentive to the embers
close to the chimney
and to listen
to listen always attentive
to three different tongues talking
a language at once fascinating
at once mysterious and known
to listen and to step in its music
in its lights and its unique
and universal shadows
to photograph
just for a second
to photograph their profiles with a glance
were it possible
to float
inside
the living room
like
a bird
in
the
tempest

Marnay-sur-Seine, France, 2002

Translated by María Teresa Borys

FIVE POEMS TO ZARABANDE OF THE DARK DEATH

IT IS THE OLD PHILIPPUS

misted over the mirror,
trying in the silence the narrowest path,
when reasons and words
have stopped burning from his mouth.
What for?
For whom?
Only a gasp.
The night as a river that bends.
The humid knife of the moon
scratching the darkness.
The faceless writing of death.
The thick fog of blood.
Saturated the hope,
Philippus of Arimathea
emerges from a fitful sleep
not yet collapsing,
like a funereal acrobat,
on the most fragile string of the heart,
where only the bitterest rasping breaths vibrate yet for him.
The man, according to Philippus,
Is a nihilist thought in God's mind.

2
REAP EVERY IMAGE

Make from language your own gallows.
Ascend heavily its stairs.
Be the executioner. Cancel the representation promptly.

3
IN VAIN HAVE I FOUGHT AGAINST THE STUBBORN INSOMNIA
of my death.
Life is an assembly of shadows
That sacrifice each other.

4
WITH WHICH OF ALL MY LOVES
shall I bribe death?
Flesh plots and conspires
from within the depth: the phlegm,
the lump drenched in grease,
the fury of dust to turn to dust.
With which of all my rusts
shall I oxidize its scythe?

5
WITHOUT FACES NOR LIMBS IT STAYS BEHIND.
The hills of my body get chilled.
My voice sinks hesitant
in the marshy heart of God.

Translated by María Teresa Borys

ARMANDO URIBE ARCE

5 POEMS

1
Death alone is chaos.
Has anyone seen a chaos?
Doesn't have legs, arms.
Death on a wheelchair.
Death, there is no point
nor luck, and you roll, roll.

2
Goodbyes are said
final. Why do you cry?
I do not find the hours
to die. And there is no point.
I march step after step
after the femmes
fatales. Why do you cry?
The gods don't love me.

3
Freeme: lazy and boring
pulling out of myself crab sparks
round beast I commit suicide
in this world, who supports me?
In this world, in this nest
you don't fit, death, in this pot.

4
And how I wish to be dead
in a dead man's suit,
with a cap and this pair
of black eyes open.

5
It is very possible that you are not
neither that nor the other
Neither this nor the one
Good bye, good bye. What's up?
What's left for me.

Translated by María Teresa Borys

JOSÉ MARÍA MEMET

THE MENTAL TIGER

In the void, only the tiger remains.
In the keen ear, there's no sound.

To listen to the carnivorous beast
walking, lost in its swaying,
descending invisible, perfect
along the lotus leaves covering the pond,
is a utopia comparable to the shadow
we exercise with the fervor of a beginner
in the art of speaking from the cage.

In the void, only the tiger moves.
In the keen ear, there's no sound from the foliage.

The feline is not domesticated, it's an enormous cat;
since it has wandered far too long
through the immensity of the mind
we think we hear roaring at night.
Those are fears, dear reader. Just clawing.

To create myths, fear is needed;
creating one
becomes indispensable.

Translated by Jorge Etcheverry, edited by Sharon Khan

COCK FIGHT

In the ring the black cock is a wonder.
The red cock is death that has been sent.

Good and evil
are abstractions.
He who bets tonight
will win for sure.

The feathered ones stand straight up.
Beaks and spurs in the air!

Amidst the spurting blood, someone shouts:
tonight the lead-gray cock is making sparks fly!
Soon a wing's dragging on the sand,
the sand is wet from the sea.

A sea of blood,
an ocean of feathers.
The tides are dragging minds along
Who's won?

The white cock
has gone, hopping to heaven.
The blue cock is looking for its wheat.
The Babel cock is strutting in colours.
The number cock is in mathematics.

Freedom is really what it seems
when a cock turns green
all the bettors
are surprised with their paint brushes.

For the world vision
to become a light in the night, strike a match.

The dead cocks will sing
when it goes out.

Translated by Jorge Etcheverry, edited by Sharon Khan

WHITE COCK ON WHITE BACKGROUND

Even if the absence of colour is real
let's remove the red that colours the cock,
let's remove its yellow feet,
the black beak,
the dried blood from its eyes.

Let's remove the landscape where it's used to wandering,
the intense green of the foliage,
let's leave in the white the white cock.

Do you see it now?
Its appearance is almost immaterial, but it's there.
Standing under this imaginary fern
singing with strength,
resplendent.

What colour is the song of the white cock now?
Is it defined by the colour of absence?

It's the task of human beings to appreciate that life exists.
The sea's enormous and life sings from the deep.

Translated by Jorge Etcheverry, edited by Sharon Khan

HISTORY OF THE NIGHT
Fragment III

In the obtuse vagrancy
of a static clock-shop, cold
and dislocated by the atom's exercise,
I open the fabrics of permanency
and unhook myself from the arteries of time,
like a wild pollen grain
that falls into the perfect omission
of an ice plain.

Imprisoned in the cells of the nation,
full of American energy,
I stay furtive
in the intestines of an imaginary pavilion,
and stalking the hosts' withdrawal
from this monastery of human greed,
I seek an armistice of absence.

After they marched away from the forge
to rest with their exchequers
and their great speeches about freedom;
in the prison's walls
martyrdom's taciturn howl remained,
exercising its discipline of outrage
over the most crumbled breast;
while sometimes,
in the ceremonial confinement,
a prisoner gets lost in the quietude
and we never see him again.

When everything is silence
and no one shouts of grief,
I take back again the patience of the annals,
and by the streak of my sovereignty
I leave on a trip.

And between the oxide of the solemn gears
and the cupola of life, I am;
and between the blackmail of the guns,
the knives and the electrodes, I am
and nothing perturbs my right to be.

Fragment VIII

In the croup of this cavity,
I try to survive an imminent distillery,
as the navigator lost
in a lightless puddle,
exposes to the oceanic benevolence of the desert
a huge false theory.

I was the pollen's witness,
who in the seasons of drought,
fainted with its fruit
from the earth's crepuscular platform;
I saw the laborious insistence of human roots,
trying to lift their monuments and falling
under the soul of the guns,
and, in my saddest journeys,
I saw, in the American suburbs, the woman
disappearing among the soot of the shacks,
and the other,

who being ugly,
became slave.

After so many exclamations
came out of the molten face of the ash,
in the corridors of my broken infancy
I survived what others could not.

And now,
in the seed-spike of this high labyrinth,
I refuse to subside like the flood waters
that are putrefying in a container without soul,
punished by forgetfulness.

If one day I leave this miserly lodging,
I would return with my voice and my hands
to the transgressed plains
to challenge the execution walls
suspended on the horizon.

Harassed by a damned syllabary,
plunged in a statue's spirit,
I live free, in the grotto of my captivity,
in love with the vestiges of other freedoms.

THE BARBIZON

The ones who speak Spanish here are kitchen helpers. They clean the carpets, wipe the bar counter. Mexicans, Guatemalans, Costa Ricans, the whole Latin American OAS, serving the bosses. Like the Mapuches in Santiago, Chile. They're little worms in the Big Apple. "Pedro, bring me a coffee", "Antonio, make me a drink." Not even the Blacks would do these menial tasks. The Uruguayans are taxi drivers in New Jersey. The Argentinians sell chocolates/fine silver crafts. Not to mention the Colombians. The Chileans are cultural attachés.
A nineteenth-century, TV set ambience, with dreadful paintings of rural scenes framing the comings and goings of the little lovers of governesses.
It means, little news from reality. Reality is these concrete walls, against which come crashing the speeches given by heads of state when they take power.
"The Barbizon," one hundred and twenty dollars a room, let's not even think who's going to benefit from the free-trade agreement. "Pedro, give me a coffee", "Antonio, make me a drink."

Translated by Jorge Etcheverry, edited by Sharon Khan

THE BEST SHOW IN CHILE

At the time I was working as a helper
at a cabaret in downtown Santiago.
At night I cleaned stains of dry semen
at a branch of the Chase Manhattan Bank
When I had to go to the urinal
I stood on my tiptoes to look through a small window

at the poster of Maggie
posted on the wall across the street.
I don't touch Maggie, not even with a rose petal,
despite all the years she's been wiggling her muff.
I respect medical science and religions
Maggie has no reason to envy
the driving forces of female volunteering.
She's the one who performs the miracle
of making the husbands of these ladies smile
Any way you look at it
Maggie's performance is far superior
to the truly sad one given daily by the judges
in the highly illustrious Court.
One night she came to the bathroom here
"the one over there is too dirty," she said.
And I myself stood watch over the door
so no son of a bitch could get in
while she was downloading.

Translated by Jorge Etcheverry, edited by Sharon Khan

XIMENA TRONCOSO

THE FLOWER OF THE POEM

The fertile woman makes of her arms
a blanket for the son of blood
to whom her womb gave birth.
The woman poet knits a nest of verses.
The heart opens
to give way to the eternity of reason.
Like a cloud flying in the eye of the earth.
The poem rises up in a message of peace
discharging the waters that calm
the heart-rending cry of her children.
The verse knits a new world
with a cluster of stars
opens the eyes of the blind man
to the freedom of the light.

Translated by Jorge Etcheverry, edited by Sharon Khan

BIRTH

There are figures outlined in the air
Steps
Men walk along the century
tinting the waist of history
rubbing knots from their bandages
touring popular verses on the street
The fraternal flame draws songs
from the mud
They ride without helmets

in magical revolutions
Their bodies engender the fury of forgetfulness
A winter sky
approaches
pierced by the golden forging of verse
A soul links another
children walk along the century
The igneous rains flow along the crust

Translated by Jorge Etcheverry, edited by Sharon Khan

POETS OF THE NORTH OF CHILE

We are poets of water within the chill of death
soaked to the skin in our open rebellion
orphans we are
orphans without names or prospect
our eyes worn out by sand and suffering.
Trees frighten us
with their terrifying green.
The rain frightens us.
The birds we know are vultures
and the vulture we love for its black despair
its funereal patience, its stench, its obsidian feathers.
We are bass drum and bronze trumpet musicians
a carnival to dull the distance.
Dunes - desert – brotherhood
brass flowers tarnishing memory.
High plains is what we are
a nowhere geography
in a country given to denying our existence.
We are poets like farmers of the void
making bread out of hope,
raising quinoa, the poetry of the night,
sucking the soul from the guayaba,
doing what we can for our country by sheer force
under the blazing sun
smelting our words from ore.
If we are lucky they mention us sometimes…
in the imagination of the South
we are half brothers,
stepchildren at the edge of the map,

bereft of all parable,
mythology of the bars,
palaver of the port.
Peruvians they call us
as if to insult...
Indians they call us
in their european fantasy.
We put poems into bottles
and throw them onto the pampas
or on the nitrate flats nostalgic for the moon.
We sit down and wait for misfortune to arrive
massacres, shipwrecks, tsunamis...
accustomed as we are to hunger and woe

Translated by Gabriela Etcheverry

ON THE CELEBRATION

Sometimes
a lone angel visits me
we break bread together
that bread handed out in prisons
and we celebrate this bread
and in silence
we drink in its crumbs of hope,
its candescent yeast
the fire
of my oven-heart
becomes a miracle.
The sacred rite concluded,
he,
the angel
flies his sacred freedom
while
over me,
the poet,
falls sacred music
falls sacred food
and I understand then
that I am the chosen one
of this "deplorable honour" of loving you.

Translated by Gabriela Etcheverry

SERMON OF THE LITTLE MAGENTA MEN
for D.T.

the donkey and death get naked
Do not forget the reader, po Po

Poe
t: the poetry reader
is the most demanding most intelligent
cultured most prepared!
Poetry is not for anyone and not
anyone writes in oils with the brush
of Francis Bacon. Recognize the limit of your
possibilities. Limit yourself to the watercolours,
in your beginnings. Draft, with
finesse. Filter, sift,
purify. Explore your vein
without depleting your mine.
The sound is in
the letter. The voice, writer, it is given
onto you.
   Do not overload. No acrobatic
sommersaults, rien de/nada de pyrotechnics. [creo que se puede dejar el
frances]
The cake of letters doesn't need icing.

Do not play your lyre for gold coins or
bronze (japanese proverb)

You shall consider

the usual: the Moon flowers death
sadness. The double articulation,
the impossible balance between vomit
and style, women of words (the Goddess),
the Muses the figures the resources; the
Usual, in other wineskins. Meditate
on your verses seven times, and on your Verb
forty times seven. Add two
plus two; discount
the VAT!

Note:
VAT= Value Added Tax

Translated by María Teresa Borys

ARS POETIQUE
for the Imaginary Gallery

May the verse be like a picklock
To enter and steal by night
To the dictionary to the light
Of a flashlight
Stone-
deaf
Wailing Wall
Licked
Walls of Ear!
a Rocket falls a Mirage passes by
the windows still shaking
We are in the age of nerves and the acronyms
and the acronyms
are the nerves, are the nerves

True strength lies in the checkbook
is the checkbook
Muscle sold in packets by Post
ambition
poetry does not rest
it is h
an
g
  in
   g
at the address of Archives and Libraries and Museums in Luxury Goods,
bare
necessities,
oh, poets! Synge yee not
to the roses, oh, allowe them to mature and make them
into musk-rose jam in the poem

Translated by María Teresa Borys

The Author begs the reader four Guineas for the trouble (Your Tips are My wagers)

ALFREDO LAVERGNE

AMERICA

North Central South
America

With vertical aventure   With your dismenbered columns
With 500 lineal years   With the oblivion they impose on you
With your petrified giants   With your chimneys of faith

Now that you have felt the hads of man and woman sowing
Now that you have been stirred by the heat and cold of your surface
Now that you have discovered your oceanic splendors
Now that you are witness to the influence of your great cities

America

People who await their land   Land which awaits its people

Continent
Of future language   Of future identity

From rainstorm to rainbow

How wise of you to have given us defenseless faces!

Translated by Hugh Hazelton

THE MULTINATIONAL

In this place
insecurity is earthly
without monastic complications.

In this place
chaos is everywhere
thoungh a few are in control.

In this place
depressions is routine
hunched up in your temples.

In this place
the failing economy has its own graph
in our consciousness and wallets.

In this place
the capitalist neither improvises
nor lets up.

In this place
automation is a banquet
for the shareholders.

In this place
the populist speaks of independence
and we work in the lines.

In this place
the social democrat smiles at us
and the company supports his reelection.

In this place
the union is underdeveloped
and officially deplores anticommunism.

In this place
every human being is a number
and I am unionized worker 87653.

Translated by Hugh Hazelton

GONZALO MILLÁN

THE CITY

37

The blind man is feeling his way.
The blind man has a very keen ear.
Sounds are perceived by the ear.
I hear whispering voices.
Whispering wind.
Whispering water.
I hear indistinct voices.
I hear undefinable sounds. I hear steps.
I hear whistling.
I hear car horns.
I hear the bustle of the street.

The blind man is groping his way.
The blind man goes by touch.
The fear is tangible.

I heard bursts of machine gun fire.
The machine guns rattled.
I heard tanks roll.
I heard airplanes fly low.
Explosions reverberated.
The explosions shattered the silence.
Then silence.
Tarara! goes the trumpet.
The sound of the trumpet is piercing.
I hear military bands.
The fife is shrill.

Boom! goes the bass drum.
I hear soldiers march.
I hear snare drums.
The drums roll.
Rat-a-tat! go the drums.
I hear bugles play.
The bugles sound shrill.
I hear shouts of command.

I lost my eyesight as a child.
I have lost the memory of my face.
The blind man counts the steps.
I hear strange noises.
I hear sobbing voices.
I hear lamenting.
I hear the whistle of a train.
I hear weeping.
You can hear the surf roar.
I hear grumbling.
I hear swearwords.
I hear moans.
I hear boisterous laughter.
I hear absurd things.
I hear panting.
The ringing of cash registers.
Squealing brakes.
A drill pierces the pavement.
The bells ring clearly.

Loose horseshoes clatter.
The wagon wheels screech.
The peasants go to market.
The merchants praise their wares.
The buyers bargain.

The street vendors hawk their goods.
I smell rubber wine fruit pears apples.
I smell anise cumin cloves.
I smell fragrant flowers.
I smell musk garlic.
I smell rancid repugnant nauseating smells.

I hear the cry of the newborn.
I hear the scream of the virgin.
I hear the gasp of the dying.

The city is an immense cave never
reached by daylight.
The city is the murmuring darkness of a great
subterranean river.
The city smells deafens hushes stinks.
The city is the tomb of the sea.
The shell to which I press my ear.
A beehive invaded by ants.
The swarms disperse and the queens nest
in my ears.

The blind man has a very keen nose.
The fishermen smell of fish.
The firemen smell of smoke.
The carpenters smell of wood.
The newspaper boys of ink.
The sick of medicine.
The gravediggers of grave.
The shoemakers of leather.
The greedy of money.
The tyrant's agents smell of rat
 The agents try to coax me.
They threaten me.

They even offer me money.
To them I am blind and mute.
Leave this poor blind man in peace.
Let me play my guitar in peace.

Translated by Annegret Nill

ARIADNA'S DISSOLUTION

Certain PLACE, uncertain hour
of the cloth of her body,
blind knot and blind rejoining
of our unconciliated saciety.

She is the nymf of the treshold.
All immidiacies, all imminences.
At the same time the claudication of my hopes
and insult to my unwary welcome.

All folds now into the silence unfurled by her skin
as the day grows her immense unctuosity
and the water from the stream unravels her cold maidenhood.

Fullness of the most predatory age
meekly oncoming to my void
where her foot advances thus to unburden itself,
the gift of her coming to untie itself,
and she to dissolve herself,
  to unstring herself,
migratory daughter,
in the smoky aftertaste of my mouth.

Translated by María Teresa Borys

GRAY ROSE

Behind the pine forest and wider,
undercover and swinging, it grew to your astonishment
throughout the long strong night
the proximity of the Sea
in a baptismal act for the eyes, for the overawement
of all your senses.
For that your instant that did not grow with you.
Behind the precinct of your sleep awaited your most impatient age
the extense age of the Water,
your first unmoveable certainty.
Those were the waters caught in full state of the word.
The body of all the findings
and its voice already close extended to meet you:
streightening against the tumultous morning
the smart position, the never dispossesed gift
of the great gray rose.

Translated by María Teresa Borys

VALLIS CLAUSA

Towards the alighting of the Cave
the clear water araises to shade herself,
the arboreal water takes in the landscape
dissolving the best of it in its reflection
The eyes pour out the best of ourselves
into their gathering:
the water's dream startled anew
torn at the centre.
We run within her answering the call of the valley
converted to the devotion that joins from age to age

the stone ark to the deeply wounded laurel
and we are one and the same voice in its clear heaviness,
twin shadow in its drippings.

Translated by María Teresa Borys

From "Altazor, or, A voyage in a parachute"

PREFACE

I was born at thirty three, the day of the death of Christ; I was born on the equinox, under the hydrangeas and the heat airplanes.

I had the deep look of a pigeon, of the tunnel and the sentimental car. I threw acrobatic sighs.

My father was blind and his hands were more admirable than the night.

I love the night, hat of every day.

The night, the night of the day, of the day the next day.

My mother talked like the dawn and like the zeppelin that's going to fall. She had hair the color of the flag and eyes full of distant ships.

One afternoon I took my parachute and said: "Between a star and two swallows". Here is death coming closer like the Earth to the falling baloon.

My mother embroidered deserted tears on the first rainbows.

And now my parachute falls asleep from sleep to sleep through the spaces of death.

On the first day I found an unknown bird that told me: "If I were a dromedary I wouldn't thirst. What time is it? It drunk the dew drops of my hair, threw me three looks and a half and left saying: "Goodbye" with his arrogant handkerchief.

Around two o'clock I found a beautiful airplane, full of scales and snails. It was looking for a nook in the sky to hide from the rain.

Far over there, all the anchored ships, in the tint of dawn. Suddenly they started to detach themselves, one by one towing like a flag shreds of the unquestionable dawn.

Next to walking away last, the dawn disappeared behind some overly inflated waves.

Then I heard the Creator talk, without name, which is a simple hole in the void, beautiful like a navel.

«I made a big noise and that noise formed the ocean and the ocean waves.

»That noise will always be attached to the sea waves and the sea waves will be attached to it, like stamps on postcards.

»Afterwards I wove a large twine of luminous rays to sew the days one by one; the days that have a legitimate and reconstructed east, however unquestionable.

»Aftarwards I traced the geography of the Earth and of the lines of the hand.

»Afterwards I drank a bit of cognac (due to the hydrography).

»Afterwards I created the mouth and the lips of the mouth, to imprison the misleading smiles and the teeth of the mouth, to guard the swearwords that come to us from the mouth.

»I created the tongue of the mouth that men deviated from its role, forcing it to learn how to speak... her, her, the beautiful swimmer, forever deviated from its aquatic and purely caressing role.»

My parachute started to fall precipitously. Such is the strength of attraction of death and the open tomb.

You can believe it, the tomb has more power than the eyes of the beloved. The open tomb with all its magnets. And I say this to you, to you whose every smile compels me to think of the beginning of the world.

My parachute got entangled on an unlit star conscientiously following its orbit as if ignoring the futility of its efforts.

And taking advantage of this well earned rest I started to fill in with deep thoughts the boxes on my slab:

«True poems are fires. Poetry propagates throughout everything, illuminating the consummations with pleasure shudders or death throes.

»Writing should be done in a language that is not the mother tongue.

»The four cardinal points are three: south and north.

»A poem is a thing that will be.

»A poem is a thing that never is but should be.

»A poem is a thing that never has been, never could be.

»Flee from extreme sublime, if you don't want to die crushed by the wind.

»If I did at least one crazy thing per year I would drive myself crazy.»

I take my parachute, and at the edge of my orbiting star I jump into the atmosphere of the last sigh.

I roll unendingly over the rocks of dreams, I roll in between the death clouds.

I meet the Virgin sitting on a rose and she tells me:

»Look at my hands: they're transparent like the light bulbs. Do you see the filaments through which the blood of my light runs intact?

»Look at my halo. Its somewhat chipped which proves my old age.

»I am the Virgin, the Virgin not blemished by human ink, the only one not halfway done, and I am the captainess of the other eleven thousand that were really too restored.

»I speak the language that fills the hearts according to the law of the communicating clouds.

»I always say goodbye and I stay.

»Love me, my son, because I love your poetry and I will show you aerial feats.

»I need so much tenderness, kiss my hair, I washed it this morning on the dawn clouds and now I want to sleep on the mattress of intermittent mist.

»My looks are a wire on the horizon, a resting place for swallows.

»Love me.»

I kneeled down on the circular space and the Virgin lifted herself up and came to sit on my parachute.

I slept and recited my most beautiful poems.

The flames of my poetry dried the Virgin's hair, who thanked me and went away sitting on her bland rose.

And here I am, alone like the small orphan of anonymous shipwrecks.

Ah, how beautiful…, how beautiful.

I see the mountains, the rivers, the jungles, the sea, the ships, the flowers and the snails.

I see the night and the day and the axis on which they join.

Ah, ah, I am Altazor, the great poet, without horse that ate birdseed, nor hot its throat with the paleness of the moon, but with my small parachute for umbrella over the planets.

From every drop of sweat from my forehead I birthed stars, that I leave onto you the work of baptizing like the wine bottles.

I see everything, I have a brain forged on prophetic tongues.

The mountain is the sigh of God, ascending in a bloated thermometer until it reaches the feet of the beloved.

Who has seen it all, who knows every secret without being Walt Whitman, because I have never had a beard as white as the beautiful nurses and the freezing cold streams.

Who hears during the night the hammers of false purses, that are only active astronomers.

Who drinks the hot glass of wisdom alter the deluge being doves and who knows the route of fatigue, the boiling wake left by ships.

Who knows the stores of memories and the beautiful forgotten stations.

He the shepherd of airplanes, the driver of lost nights and of the trained wests towards the unique poles.

His groan is similar to a blinking net of meteorites without witness.

The day lifts in his heart and he lowers the eyelids to make the night of the agricultural rest.

He washes his hands in the sight of God and brushes his hair like the light and harvests those thin ears of satisfied rain.

The shouts go away like the herd over the hills when the stars sleep alter a night of continuos work.

The beautiful hunter in front of the celestial drinking through for birds without heart.

Be sad like the gazelles facing the infinite and the meteorites, like the desserts without mirages.

Until the arrival of a mouth swollen with kisses to the wine harvest of the dessert.

Be sad for she awaits you in a corner of this year that ends.

This perhaps extreme of your next song and will be beautiful like the free fall and rich like the equatorial line.

Be sad, sadder than the rose, the beautiful cage of our looks and of the inexperienced bees.

Life is a trip on parachute and not what you want to believe.

Let us fall, fall off our zenith to our nadir and let us leave the air stained with blood to poison those who will come tomorrow to breathe it.

Within yourself, outside of yourself you will fall from the zenith to the nadir because this is your destiny, your miserable destiny. And the taller you fall the taller will be the bounce, the longer your duration in the memory of the stone.

We have jumped off our mother's womb or off the edge of a star and we are falling.

Ah my parachute, the only perfumed rose of the atmosphere, the death rose, falling headlong among the stars of death.

Have you heard? This is the sinister noise of the closed breasts.

Open the door to your soul and go out to breathe to the side outside. You can open with a sigh the door the hurricane might have closed.

Man, here is your parachute wonderful like vertigo.

Poet, here is your parachute wonderful like the magnet of the abyss.

Mage, here is your parachute that one word of yours can turn into a paralift wonderful as the ray that would like to blind the creator.

What are you waiting for?

But here is the secret of the Dark that forgot to smile.

And the parachute awaits tied to the door like the horse of the never ending escape.

Translated by María Teresa Borys

THE BOA

According to the luminescent billboard of the subway terminus it was 16:00 hours, the temperature was 32°C and rising, the skies were clear.
The train was stopped at *Secret Street* station. Its final destination was *Dark Runs The Blood Street* station. Its silent breathing allowed it to go unnoticed. Some passengers began to board through the innocuous doors of the swift rolling serpent. In its palpitating heart of threatening mouths the dangerous boa that transported men guiding itself by the map of life and death, scanned the area.

The Boa
Inside, frustrations and obsessions, curses and anguishes, anxieties and fears took their places in the rows of naked seats. Cigarettes in their mouths, alcohol bottles in their coat pockets, the yellowish and the translucent, the hot and the burning. The pickpockets eyed the unwary victims, womanizers ogled naked asses, babies suckled, others cried.

The Boa
The train slowly started its vertiginous race down the abyss, the images through the windows, the posters on the walls, the advertisements, the subway maps, the Coca Cola smiles, all became blurred.
Inside, the people devoured open newspapers, the classified ads and the perverse malignant news of the tragedy-peddlers.

The Boa
The train picked up speed.

The tunnels flitted by minute after minute, short and long tunnels like daydreams' tides that started and ended prematurely. Short and long, tunnels of life, tunnels of death. A decrepit old man and a precocious young boy kissed pictures of naked girls in Penthouses and Playboys, little girls ran inside each car.

The Boa
The decomposing mass of flesh slowly started to show signs of mobility as if agitated by the proximity of the next stop.
Preparing. *The Boa*
The hermetically sealed windows, the electronically closed doors, the interior atmosphere dry and thick. The train began internal contractions, its intestinal fluids, the efficient gastric juices started to feel their catch, to savour it, the cars underwent a metamorphosis, closing in on the passengers, squeezing them into a shapeless digestible pulp. The delicately complex intestinal juices began a devastating and demolishing action inundating all the cars, dissipating and dissolving the frustrations and obsessions, the curses and the anguishes, the anxieties and fears, the cigarettes and the bottles, the shapes of the past.

All was silence, calm, peace and relaxation. One could imagine the sun on the surface burning the terrain under which the subway train prowled in the shadows of life and death.

The cars returned to their original state, the train slowed, approaching the station. When the subway train made its stop there was nothing but impeccable empty seats, *Express*. Nobody disembarked through those doors that opened to receive passengers who entered one by one, by the dozens, hundreds,
more than two thousand.

Girls of short skirts flirted with stylish men. Boys passed by selling candies and cigarettes, dark men sat crammed, passing the time, watching other passengers. And the obsessions and the fears and the anguish and the desire to arrive soon at the next station showed themselves once again on the hundredth turn of the subway train that summer afternoon of July 24th, 1997 when the savage boa, the wheeled serpent transported the men like a Muse inspiring the future, guiding itself by the map of life and death.

Translated by Roxane Pitre

JOSÉ ÁNGEL CUEVAS

III
LET ME DIE AS I'VE LIVED *(fragments from Proyecto de país)*

He practically lived in this café
Jorge Etcheverry

people like to hear crying
and I can do it in a really intense way
Rodrigo Lira

I NEVER GOT OUT OF THAT HORRIFIC CHILE

5.3.1
Oh, to find yourself in a Great Redemption
like Niky S.' Instantaneous Train
a train penetrated by artichoke-covered houses
blanketed by the world, that's there
/to find yourself thrown into a police station
like a piece of shit
thinking about your small kids in Apartment 408
and J. Lennon shot/also a posteriori
Life's a Bitch,
getting shot so often
getting shot so often/
those were the prophecies.

5.3.4

What they wanted was a Happy World
or a happy family, a happy marriage/
and last but not least, a happy guy,
his roasted chicken, his drink
Living his life.

5.3.5

What was your project for a country,
the beauty and brightness of the stars,
the clearness and splendor of its skies,
with reasonable people/without inferiority complexes,
without tsunamis, and lots of love
for your fellow man?

From the Sons of Tarapacá Club, I tell you:

when this enormous wound heals,
in the successive transformations that could come
I would only be
a guy full of marks/
a one-armed guy/
but, who cares, if the Grave
swallows once and again. It's going to open
the enormous mouth/the Lone Star/
it's going to take charge of its brilliant skies,
take from itself the provincial streets/
because for motherlands life goes by in another way.

I know that one was he who was going to build this Country.

But, I don't know who I am,

my father told me: don't worry about a thing
only about yourself,
because when you land in shit
nobody's going to give you a hand,
and he sang to me *"yira, yira"/*
then I saw the flag flutter
I became aware, as they said/
and fought against the tremendous
block of rock, mud, manure.
The rest, everyone knows.

6.1
So what, is love going to be made on these beaches,
if the comrade comes later on/with his thirst for power,
and with his so-called dominance/ doesn't let anybody speak/
and doesn't call free/secret ballot/informed elections?

GREAT COMMUNITIES OF DECENT PEOPLE

easy-going people/people from the South/

to live with good people,
the ones from this Sea of People/this density
that devours you.
A screen filled with love affaires/

This scenario should be disseminated/
let these communes be taken to the Desert
to share their blue screen
 along the Country,
let the Fields come back

they should go, so go!
register yourself in the Office of Returnees,
go/I'm staying.

And to begin a new life.

7.1.3
The deserts will grow in our hearts
Maribel Tapia thinks she's Marilyn
she dyed her hair blond and her firm tits,
they did an electroencephalogram
her person was an island.
But it was a very bad force, her person/

But then again:
there's the possibility of great parties in the sky/
feeling you're being carried away by the instruments
climbing a mountain, covering the universe
under the blankets.

7.2
A happy outcome to negotiations should be reached concerning
the award of damages to the personnel of the motherland
Pensions calculated, based on/
the average income in the scale of salaries and wages
of the Republic.

(BUT IF THE REGIMENTS TAKE TO THE STREET
the regiments will completely take over life/
from then on transmissions/
will be suspended/everything will totally change/
for an eternity/until further notice)

Hey, keep on travelling/to start a family/
still under the rattle of machine gun fire
the silence of dead cities
that would come!

Translated by Jorge Etcheverry, edited by Sharon Khan

JAIME GÓMEZ-ROGERS

THE MAGICIAN

In any case
Aunty Mamma went away like the ducks
to the South
tied up in her wooden box.
The organ breathing heavily
among plastic flowers
took its last breath
with dignity
in the presence of the notary
with dignity inherited by the others.

 Here we have the poet, the little poet.
Aunty Mamma
tell him to climb
yes
tell him to climb on the kitchen table
to recite three short poems
and a longer one afterwards
if he wants
(after we leave)
Do you know the one that starts "With the rain…"
and I don't know what else?
Tell him Aunty Mamma, tell him
"with the rain"

From the heights, my voice
will descend warm and thick
like the voice of cool actors.
and after "that,"

everybody goes crazy clapping.
I shrug my shoulders:
Sometimes,
faced with death I'd prefer to shut up
But all of this is gone,
little by little
left somewhere (among the papers)
in some drawer
—look for it—
the photo taken by *flaco* Acevedo.
The last time
I decided to go and die somewhere else.

One afternoon I went up San Cristóbal hill.
I stayed at the zoo for four years disguised as a buffalo.
Chewing the herbs, I went unnoticed
But one day a visitor from a province caught me
 then things came to an end—
I was trying to fry an egg in a corner of the cage
(I never should have done it)
He shouted.
He told the Manager on me
the son of a bitch.
Someone came,
then somebody else,
then they threw stones at me.
And speeches.
At first I tried to get smart.
Then I had to run.
I ran to the hut of the funicular
I saw the roofs of the houses getting closer.
I was going back to the city
that scared me so much
Going back.

Forgetting Tomás (my four-footed name).

Down there things
haven't changed that much.
In the cage
every bit of the familiar life was left behind:
my latest poems,
Father's boots,
an orange tree,
an address book
and my running shoes.
I kept the beard for a while
the shyness of a buffalo
and a slight "tic" in the ears.

I felt like a new coat.
But,
I got used to it.

My footprints in the park were damp.
Things, I say,
hadn't changed that much.
The leaves fell in autumn.
The river kept roaring down the slope.
The light
lingered in a crack in the cement.
Not to make conceited interpretations
I'm only sticking to the choreography.
Everybody ran in the rain with black umbrellas,
shoes
and leather briefcases.

We were superstitious to the bone.

Translated by Jorge Etcheverry, edited by Sharon Khan

OMAR CID

AND YOU?

It wasn't easy
he says
without moving a muscle
and repeating his litany:
Miguel Enríquez is dead.
The worker Juan Alegría Mondaca
 who had nothing to do with it
got it too.
Ricardo Valenzuela
fell, shot in the back.
Juan Waldemar Henríquez,
died in combat.
And you,
who talked so much about the class struggle,
have been made manager, adviser and lobbyist.

Translated by Jorge Etcheverry, edited by Sharon Khan

SONG OF PRAISE TO THE OFFICE

They look at me with mistrust
They're right
I've been with you
since Operation Return.
I saw some
grow up
others
grow old.

I followed their trials
with a shyster's passion.
I knew their families
we shared tea and bread.
They never understood
revolution
as a cancelled project.
They had to be infiltrated
and new jails had to be invented
to defend democracy

Translated by Jorge Etcheverry, edited by Sharon Khan

(INTERNAL) ENEMY

Sentenced to silence
the (internal) enemies
live dreaming
of rebellion and crisis.
They infect the streets
with their lost causes.
All this
because of their eagerness
to stick chewing gum in buses
to pinch the bums of Lady Ministers.
They adopt an air of indigenous rights activists
they draw the hammer and sickle
in a country where these tools
have become obsolete.
The enemies,
says an informer,
spoil inaugurations
by shoving placards

in front of the cameras.
Just as the scissors
are about to cut the ribbon.

Translated by Jorge Etcheverry, edited by Sharon Khan

INTERFERENCES IN SITU

I

Coltrane rebounds on the
dried-up frontiers of the bar
while a young fan
Morticia-style
incorporates into the scene
the silent anachronism of one
condemned to death.
Ruby red lips
of Cinderellas as pale
as though conceived by
mimes.

I situate myself mentally
and cannot avoid the eyes
almond-shaped and dark
of a brightness similar perhaps
only to a
        sunrise
eyes that from time to time cross
on line
my coordinates
after the rain
after the eyes
inevitably
her entire face
and at this point
everything ceases to be valid.

I smile with her smile and
amidst the jazz
her tiny voice in
a half tongue tells
a story tinted
with the magic of
Francisca.

As if I had her in front of me
right now
her brilliant pearls watch me
and I'm happy they're not from her landscape
those who scribble
other stories in the sand
or on the missiles and bombs
in the Middle East.

II

Those children who
wanting to make non-existence
disappear
playing at understanding the war
and I am glad, Francisca,
that you are not hidden right now
in some shelter
without waiting for tomorrow
subject to tactical discipline,
but your coming
and going according to my mood
hand in hand with Parker now,
while
I turn the slow cup

and its longing.
What a strange thing, Chiquita,
life brought us together here, in this
knot of frontiers and blood
we should be thankful
I say
because you are not in
the other landscape,
the one that I can only reach
through the screen
and I confess
   that sometimes
      I lose my courage
I press the magic key
and I escape discreetly
among anodyne frequencies
and it happens that some days
I fall for the playful glance of
an imaginary prince
vainly attempting
to escape the seduction of leaving.

Another cup
taciturn accomplice of my nights
and from there
I abandon this tête-à-tête
with my orphan other
upon returning home
to watch the midnight news
to be happy again
that you are not in them Francisca.
The problem is
we believe we are gods

envious
we emulate the carpenter
without the audacity of dying
we forget we were engendered among
tongues and caresses
 to turn ourselves into part-time puppets
evading
        if it exists
                the judgment
evading the shadows that
burst into the Santiago nights
offering roses in the pubs
or to the ones that lie shrouded
under the bridge.

They're not at the bar
neither are the bombs that suppress
the breath of Palestinian children
nor pimps who lie in wait
at the street corners
neither you, Francisca,
who'll sleep calmly for sure
given to your well-deserved dreams
while I
give myself to the passion of a sax solo
that even now
 is kidnapping
my vertices

And what does it matter
if I let myself be carried away
if everything comes together at the end of days?

One day I'll feel like forgetting

because life dresses up in nuances
and poetry is
       history.

III

At the brink of sanity
the abandonment.
Here we are, little one,
leaving you an unfinished
Da Vinci canvas
one of those that crosses the wasteland
whose glance is a mystery
loudly voiced
and leaving you as a legacy
an irremediable curse
that wanders the streets
and whose intentions are
the mystery of a story by Wells.
Poetry gives breadth
to the scene
you must be prepared
she dances on an invisible thread
and you will learn of her silhouette
in a narration by Borges
or in a Humphrey Bogart kind of glance
that a man you wouldn't know
will dedicate to the women in a bar.
Everything
is
suspended
history has decided that
it has to happen like that at least for now and
it would be fair to abandon for a few hours

the offensives that inhabit us.
Reality doesn't shelter us under cloaks
rather
it exiles us outdoors, naked
each morning
like pieces in an enormous chess game
with the sole purpose of keeping us
in this accursed game.
Rebellion,
Francisca,
draws the nuances
on the canvasses of artists.
I conjure you up
to sleep for a hundred years
to awaken in another story
with a better plot
where poetry would be the pulse
of the characters who act
then things would change
and this bad novel would remain
trapped inside a nameless book.
You will find a piece by Miles
distilled by the city walls
and in this quest you will undertake
(the one in your own dreams)
you will not be silenced by missiles
with drawings
by other child guerrillas.
So be it.

Translated by Jorge Etcheverry, edited by Sharon Khan

CLAUDIO DURÁN

CHILDHOOD AND EXILE

Introduction

How much city, ex-mine and post-mine
almost mine now, this part of you
 when silence submerges itself
into your flesh.
I walk through your silence, then
I do not recognize voices, faces are obscured
during the day rain falls though the alleys
of my memories in heavy sorrow.
City, tell me that you still
have earth for me
that my cells have a place
in ancestral soil.
Santiago, I carry your landmarks on my skin
and nonetheless, old corners have left me
like birds in winter,
the yellow flowers of your hills are there
but I can not see them as a dwelling
where are you hiding, Santiago
where are you really
in which streets or boulevards or hills
are you hiding from me?
Santiago, when night fog falls
upon the snow and then my eyes remember
what does not exist,
from the line of my circumspect family
the respite in your gaze is born:
you are the region that presides over

an Esperanto of geography:
you are in me what now is not:
Neither the language soft or harsh
at irreverent cocktails parties
 nor the soft movement of the hills
in the hot fog of summer.
I was your gaze
I was your smile
every Sunday morning
I went to your aristocratic churches
and in the evening to your notorious parties
I had drunk wine without expecting anything
 you were in me
what I was in you
Sunday after Sunday.
But, the blood that boiled in your flesh
took me from the sun to cold and to hunger.
Today I drink white snow
and the longitude of your destiny
shows me that in you
I will not be again just another citizen.
City, city
 you stopped loving me when I left,
I did not return to you for fear of death
death pierced my skin
and stopped there
and you, city, told me
that not to die then
was the same as not to be in you.
And that way the streets and horseshoes of your bicycles
left my eyes through the black labyrinth
of insomnia
and nights preceded years
and the river water that inundates the aromo trees

left my thirst for a decade
and I did not have the certainty of your hills
nor the white distance of your seasons
and the roads of my adolescent inertia
were no longer in your movements and
I followed other routes in silence.

Translated by Francisca Durán

BIRD'S REQUIEM

The cataclysm opens the doors of this city where
        Death crouches
from his universe someone attempts to take out
a sea snail   or an old starfish
The neighborhood maintains its impassive calm
        searches for itself in the glances
in the desperate need for the accomplice
not to talk
To whom it now falls to recognize the earth
the depth of the furrow that avidly opens
        its black mouth
There are trees that raise their complaining crowns
        to the heights
birds that warble to the dawn with pathetic sadness
Persepolis in ruins fills up with gases
The gardens of our Babylon drown
        in the malevolence of the air
we breathe the city from inside with fraternal simplicity

There are pains that cling frightfully to the dignity of the flesh
children's steps that lose the lucidity of balance
With punishment the skeleton loses its bony fragility
the genes break down their responsible judgment
A root impatiently penetrates into the earth's humid fertility
Every real man loses the virtue
of being a real man
in the dirty air that rarifies the corners of his soul
The day darkens for me   the night appears eternal
in the eclipse brought about by the intransigent domain

    of the machines
chimneys expelling smoke
I cough from morning to night to clear
my sternum and lungs
My mind becomes irritated, my eyesight cloudy
Upon waking in the morning I am the saddest dweller
of the planet
I fear the opacity that dawn will bring with her
Do not confuse me because I know the sky has holes
drops that resonate with a deep echo
impacting on the squalor of my brain

There are noises that make life peregrinate through memory
as if the roar of a plane that had broken the sound barrier
had put them at the threshold of the horizon
in the distance memories interfere with one another
      raindrops that cannot find the soil
A deadly soot punishes us
The sky drips deeply from within
there is no life but the one I carry on my shoulders
  on this long road
There is no humanity but the one that puts a stop
To human death

Translated by Jorge Etcheverry, edited by Sharon Khan

MATINALIS

emerged from the bed with naked loins thighs
  hairy pubis
absorbed bashful
somnolent in appearance blond
in the wavy hair of the morning

the bed still undone with morning fluids
       in the lodge
sexual odours   the sudden continuous yawns
on the stool the lingerie the perfumed panties
       and under the bed
the Saturnine darkness at an end
in the bar of dawn the smoke of my pipe
wafted arrogantly
also assigned with the aroma of tobacco,
your womb was left
including the astragalus
even better in the fibula in a fecund intrusion
Amnesty comes in the amniotic morning
the watery bloodshot eyes
perfectly embedded in the bags beneath them
the throat raw
the muscles numb
and you in the shower with no blemishes

Translated by Jorge Etcheverry, edited by Sharon Khan

JORGE ETCHEVERRY

ODE TO GRETA GARBO

The season of the skylark ceasing to whisper along telephone lines, causing person-to-person calls to flourish and sing, ceasing to whisper in the background of female voices when they answer in whatever language or sing on the other end of the line. The most satisfied men are the least productive. For the time being we find ourselves given to the description of very particular matters. What can we do? We didn't invent the world or history.

All the disheveled and aging travelling we elaborate like a spider or a snail. At this precise moment a thin young man of indeterminate age passes by, smoking. While the afternoon arches itself like the back of a white cat that grabs the orange of the world and bites hard. Like an imaginary mouth I lift those full, silky skirts. I pull down your gaudy, violet-pink stockings and nibble your slender sex, covered in soft down, the other extreme, the reason for your mouth.

You were able to annul the dimension of your poor brain, always inclined to take flight, besieged by the fragile weaving of the body's skeleton. Caged in the old familiar tales about the WHITE KNIGHT, the taste for sex, the tedium, the tendency to oversleep.

The wit of your laughter and the voracity of your eyes and fingers rise up like a butterfly with heavy velvet wings. Here, in these latitudes, frustration turns us into consumers: how many packs of cigarettes, how many cups of coffee have crashed against my lungs and liver together with the juices of your inexpressible cunt, shaking the firm, methodical meshing of the revolutionary world order, uneven and combined? Like a flourishing of faces and arms that burst into the apartment of the so-called INNER LIFE.

A swarm of bloodied lithographic paper attacks us and
makes us teeter at the corner, when we're already walking along, shaky
from tobacco and booze, and the daydreams over which you reign like
a Greta Garbo in the celluloid of the twenties, unchallenged and
unchallengeable, lifting a white thigh trimmed with a black garter
beneath the frills of a short black can-can skirt. Let your publicized
silhouette and face publicizing brassieres and dresses, the upright high
heel of the shoe, the top hat and the platinum-blonde hair be like a
candle at night in the middle of a pasture that attracts and sets fire to
all the insects on television and the hidden longings (not just ours),
that suffocates and clouds Revolutions & Humanism, that relativizes
and shapes Aesthetics & Epistemologies. With a flustered expression of
the eyes, a fluttering of the eyelashes, a short phrase in bad French.

Translated by JorgeEtcheverry and Sharon Khan.

LET THE BAND PLAY ON

It doesn't matter
Let the band play on
even if the musicians are tired
even if everyone's distracted
even if no one gives a damn
let it play on
Let the musicians wipe away the sweat
even if no one gives them any wine
even if no one gives them a glass of water
with all this heat
Let them go on
even if they're starving
even if their stomachs are growling
"We're artists after all"
one of them says
even if no one laughs at their jokes
 that are a bit stale
anyway

We have to go on
Come on boys, get up
We have to keep on playing
even if they're a bunch of losers
Let's go
let's go on
let the band play on
let it play on

Translated by Jorge Etcheverry, Edited by Nika Khan

THE HUASO OF LICANTÉN DRIVES HIS INFINITY AGAINST THE HURRICANE OF THE ORIGINS

Everything is one, one is everything and it works, raised against its image, nevertheless, I exist because I write, I am unique, uniquely unique, and therein lies the tragedy, that is the slaughterhouse of all the bells,

and my behaviour is my horse, yes, screaming, like a wounded walnut tree, among the great bayonets.

Integral, categorical, ecumenical, I need to bellow dithyrambs and mathematics, to say the national God that contains a deposit of petroleum, whose throat is horribly slit, who is sweating horror and worms,

and the rainy leonine shadow, which is far behind matter,

the dazzle of unity that spurts a jet of blood,
        inside the lungs of the world, inside, dark, of the agony of the geological hope, deep inside the original swamps,

the guttural truth of the caves of poetry, filthily infinite.

My abyss is at war with my abyss,

and my sorrow, with the dove of Humanity, with its dog-origin,

against the Gods, idiotic with illuminations, figure without trumpets, of which I am the great cadaver.
Walking, I'm going walking, walking myself,

pursuing myself, like someone biting off his head, dramatically, like someone biting off his own flags,

like someone biting the red and ardent column that grows out of him and hurts his infinite,

with its great tempest of blood;

my style bursts into an indescribable occurrence, its development matures, faces the anguished construction of the extraordinary; brought up with flashes of lightning, I come back to immortality, staring fixedly,

And I came back to the people of fire, in whom a circle gravitates that becomes inaccessible;

Then, a vulture comes out of the muzzle of God, or a terrible pig, as black as milk, from this huge furious world-class bed, in which I am sowing great soldiers killed by the jawbone of Cain, and

two skeletons that look like white lilies emigrate, flying,

or houses that rest or rabid stones that attack biting a little bird

or moons for rent

or eagles that drive yellow oxen.

A large sepulchral stone bellows in my heart, century after century, the anguish of having the head severed the honour of speaking a language that only the unfortunate understand, the sorrow and the rage of having neither sorrow nor rage, but rather an iron lion, tied up to a fallen statue,

and a crucified sun, dead set in the middle of the mouth.

Yes, temporal age puts me between the beds and their gallows, but I am as old as the world, and tall and wide like the world, and like the world, I have wicked beards on fire, I roared

like an ancient bull, when I was being born and I was coming back from eternity,

completely naked;

Nevertheless, vine arbours and shoots grow from my hide, or those tremendous ashes of Shakespeare

that roar in every shipwreck, among capsizing poets;

because one is as eternal as the handle of a knife, or as eternal as one's shirt or courage, but,

but the drum of one's chest is ripped open in the midst of red gunpowder.

Eating wounded rifles and strange jam of shoes, I travel screaming,

with a hurricane stuck in the gullet,
and a red flag, brandished like a revolver, or the head of my enemy.

I saddle up my orangutan pony and at a gallop from my saddle I can make out

eternity and its shores,

I take out the lasso and rope the animal of the world,

and in a duet of guitars the spurs sing to me the universal tune of the slaughterhouses; my grandfather was a cadaver, from whom many rivers flowed and a big black lantern tree,

I was born from the cornered maize in the sarcophagus of a Pharaoh, who fought against the Egyptian lion, and I was breastfed

by three widow snakes, extremely fond of cards;

Like beloved burning *ulpos** of fire water with dynamite, in wide jars of *Palo de sapo*,**

and I sleep on aboriginal mattresses, among sepulchers and levers,

embracing a hundred-year-old mountain to whom I've been married for two-and- a- half millennia;

I will die when my shape runs out, definitely,

and I can no longer give it to myself with my rifle of sad universal males, and a flower with a canopy of fire

because I will be hanging myself beforehand;
I am soldier of the regiment of day labourers and foreign gravediggers,

I am an official shooter of poetry,

I am the patriarch De Rokha, founder of tribes and conductor, tetrarch of a pirate clan,

a real man of the working class;

I prefer to be a cowboy than to be Marshall in the Legion of Honour of Mesopotamia,

to be a pig rather than a flowery genius, or an impostor inside the literature that is fed with little birds of sugar, and to be a second-hand sun, God or a melancholy executioner,

to be a divinoide asteroid artist, blossoming in lacunae lagoons;

I handle my rustler's axe and my philosophy teacher's lighthouse,

with sacred national terror, binging

in all the inns and taverns of Spanish antiquity;

I have a tank tied to a flag, how it roars! how it screeches!,

and how it howls!, licking the guffaws of the hundred gasoline-driven condors

keeping watch over my large cavern,

when I leave to hunt guitars with my shotgun of white lilies!;
if I declare it's because I know and because I differentiate and because I am who I am, among the poets, and because…
why is my heart a barrel of pity accused of being an assassin?

Yes, I understand perfectly, in the vicinity of this moaning ocean that's frightening;

eating roasted wine, I live inside the eternal wind,

against my symbols bounces the sacred rage of nature, and I gravitate

with my shark loneliness in my left hand;

since I am an astrologist and the national anthem grows between my teeth,

I give off so much smoke, like a big evergreen oak

and I roar, throwing myself, against the pregnant stones of the sky.

* *cold drink made with toasted flower and sugar*
** *Piscidia grandifolia*

Translated by Jorge Etcheverry, edited by Sharon Khan

ROSAMEL DEL VALLE

FROM *BLACK AND WHITE COUNTRY* (1929),

The wind swells like an old refrain.
It touches the soft branches of a tree then seems to burst.
I fend the wind off to divert it round the opening rose.
A newborn rose, it sways on its branch like a sigh.
But with a brisk martial air the wind whirls.
Its horn resounds at times with the whine of a bullet.
But the strong dancer seeks out a frail place for its repose.
How well it would sleep on the tongue of this rose open in surprise to
the breaths unknown. How well his old cascading music would flow.
I see its smile in slices and its feet climbing the void.
My heart is bent low by countless forgotten memories. The admiral of
squadrons and invisible seas, how does one sleep amid the sound of the
waves? And the sweet violence of all the storms within? At the ocean
centre like a shipwrecked hand? And up on the golden waves of the
clouds? I know that scent. I have borne it for days and nights about my
head. I have cradled it like the memory of one of the women I have
lost. I have fed it on sprightly lighting and polar flowers more beautiful
than the rain. And suddenly these things appear that I have never lost.
My heart admired once the skin of those ageless regions where echoes
seek their refuge.

But the wind has seemed to me somehow strange since I was a child. I
have seen it drift along at the measured pace of my first steps and my
first words of surprise. Imagine a tree seen for the first time, the first
tree in the world seen for the first time. The first tree and the first bird.
The first bird and the first cloud. The first cloud and the first rain. The
first rain and the first rainbow. The first rainbow and the first blue sky.
And all this—and other marvels besides, now catalogued—in the first
look at the world. And then the great wind wafting its perfume of

invisible waves. I do not recall that I ever lost these things, but how can I see them again, feel them, understand them as I did in my first encounter with them? Time has passed over my head like a fish wriggling its too-lively tail. But I take pleasure in looking back at that which I have not lost but which, albeit smaller, follows along at my side.

And behold the first dream tree solitary and green breaching the sky. The castaway sighs of my veins flow lizard-like up through its branches. It is my eyes that feed the dream of the tree while over its crown shines the song of the birds.

But one look of mine was the first story that its leaves ever heard. And from that time on the tree, the cloud, the rain, the ocean, etc. have never been sad. Never have they resembled the waterfalls that cascade down from the eyes of man.

Translated by Gabriela Etcheverry

LUCIANO DÍAZ

THE LAKES AND PRAIRIES OF CANADA

They kicked my door in
and dragged me out of the house.
I thought they were going to beat me,
in desperation I asked them: "Where are you taking me?"
 "There," said one of them,
"to the lakes and prairies of Canada..."

When I stepped down, in desperation,
I asked him:
"Sir, will I ever find peace?"
"Sure" he said,
"on the lakes and prairies of Canada..."

They came towards me
and asked me:
"Who are you, where do you come from?"
I thought they were going to beat me; in desperation
I answered:
"I am from Chile...," only then did they cool down
and told me:
"Oh, you'll find love and peace right here,
on the lakes and prairies of Canada..."

The lakes and prairies of Canada
opened their arms and hearts, offering
love and peace to me,
but pollution and drought
turned their offer into a sterile promise:
love and peace seemed out of reach for me

a broken and desperate man.

"Hey Luciano" they shouted,
"have you found love and peace yet?"
"Please, don't laugh," I said,
 "after all these years, among
drought and pollution,
even with taxes and bureaucracy, and my
 desperation and sense of loss,
I'm sure I will find peace and love some day
on the lakes and prairies of Canada,
in the country of Canada."

Traslated by Luciano Díaz

THE CAT
for Jorge Etcheverry

The cat stares
 distrustful
a loner, independent
the owner of the hours.

... He would get tired of the heat
then he would sit to smoke a cigarette.
In the world of movements
he moved with sobriety, control.
Everything at its own time.
Winter is never too rough
a pair of boots and a leather jacket
a pack of cigarettes and a bottle of red wine
Writing, painting
his woman...

The cat sleeps little
sees well at night
but is confused in the fog.
The cat always lands on its feet.

The cat crouches and then attacks
Whatever anybody says
the cat has never been domesticated.

Translated by Luciano Díaz

OLD GRAMOPHONE

Not to confuse flies with stars:
oh, the old sophist gramophone.
Kill, kill the poets to study them.
Eat, continue to eat bibliography.
Books and books, books all the way up to the clouds,
but poetry writes itself.
It is written with teeth, with danger,
with the terrible truth of each thing.
There is no worthy process, no theory,
to stop the time that sweeps us over.
The planet and the immovable dead fly and fly,
and only the wind of the Word!
What do you think of the record of the infused:
pages and more pages of cement.
Let the professors enter with their guitars
and the originalist with his fifteen fingers.
The record bearer roams and you go around
discovering the principle of principles.
The same alphabet stops short
to say the same that has been said.
And if the shoe fits put it on
before we leave you ugly and naked.
To come down from the horse. The thing starts
with the most abstract being. Or the most abstruse.
Going on and on about the strata and the structure
when the sea is demonstrated by swimming.
Always they will come without having gone
never anywhere the doctorates.
And given that they fly free: so much prestige,

so much arrogant together, so much congress.
Magazines and magazines and majesties
when the erudites put an egg.
Put an empty egg so husserline,
so sibilinamously heideggerian,
that, exhaustive and all, the hermeneuts
leave the most entwined labyrinth.
Stop, stop the music of this prose:
old the old trap of the sophists.
To the masked and to the masqueraders
this red cauterization of poetry.
De *Contra la muerte*, 1964.

Translated by María Teresa Borys

CONTRA LA MUERTE

Every day I gouge out of myself the visions and the eyes.
I don't want to see, I can't! See men die every day.
I prefer to be of stone, in the dark,
to bearing the nausea of softening from within and smiling
right and left as long as my business prospers.
I have no other business that to be here telling the truth
in the middle of the street and to the four winds:
the truth of being alive, only alive,
with feet on the ground and a free skeleton on this world.
What do we get from jumping all the way up to the sun with our machines?
at the speed of thought, hell: what do we get
with flying beyond infinity
if we continue to die without any hope of one time living
outside of the dark time?
I don't have a use for God. I don't have any use for anybody.

But I breathe, and how, and I even sleep
thinking that I have ten or twenty years to go
falling flat on my face like everyone, to sleep in two meters of cement
down there.
I don't cry, I don't cry myself. Everything will be as it should be,
but I can't see caskets and caskets
pass by, pass by, pass by, pass by every minute
full of something, filled with something, I can't see
the blood still warm in the caskets.
I touch this rose, I kiss its petals, I adore
life, I don't tire of loving women: my nourishment
is opening the world in them. But it is all useless,
because I myself am a useless head
ready for the cutting, for not understanding what is it
with waiting for another world from this world.
They talk to me of God or they talk to me of History. I laugh
at going to search so far away to explain the hunger
that devours me, the hunger for living like the sun
by the grace of the air, eternally.

De *Contra la muerte*, 1964.

Translated by María Teresa Borys

LET'S PLAY THE GREAT GAME

Let's play the great game of flying
in this chair: the world is a lightning.
I enter in Beijing and I fall headfirst into the Thames.
I sleep in the Etruscan tomb of Tarquinia.
I cut my foot in Caracas if I search for you in Paris
and I wake up bleeding on a New York dock.
But if I manage to open the prettiest girl

in Prague, the wind carries her away in Venice.
Archangels and sputniks jump into the frenzy
and my brains explode. Leave me in Buenos Aires.
All in all is in Mexico that starts in Moscow
and in the round, in one shot, I arrive to Valparaíso.
De *Contra la muerte*, 1964.

Translated by María Teresa Borys

NAÍN NÓMEZ

AFTER A LONG VOYAGE

It's not that the emotional order has lost its fierceness in this country
nor have the snows dissolved these minute stories assembled
by memory in fits and starts
It's not that the medieval castles to the south have been deserted
nor that the feudal knights insult damsels at the edge of their own dream
It's not, finally, that we, citizens of the world and owners of a non-existent country
do not respect the timid magic of these blond giants
their way of asking for things which is almost a punishment
those dogs that whirl like doves through carpeted houses
that discussion that hardly ever begins
that oblivion of the outlines of the wind

Of all this time
that is to say, of all this air that has circulated freely from one side of
my body to the other all these years
either you are mistaken and in reality
we have been words, roots, feelings that became entangled at random
in the mirrors
whatever it may have been (even a postcard scene, a puddle, a coin)
whatever it may have been, I say
this liquid cellar that fades like a monstrous leap into our nights
has brought us to this occupation as travellers pursued
in this fear of consuming its treasures moon by moon

Or did we have nothing?
Or was that vertiginous reality nothing but fossils and deception?

In this land people rest in summer and shut themselves up in Winter
children are born to be happy
cracks are closed up with great blocks of cement   '
and one sinks into a language in which beauty is something exotic

It's not that
Of all the time
that I have tried to keep under lock and key in my papers
(you'll say it's not true; the hand, touch, the lip)
though we know the minutes shatter and no glue will mend them
and still from that sand falling, from that blaze catching fire

I wonder, about this life, watered down and whitening
if what is left will serve to answer this call
to begin to fit together these stones, these buried transparencies
if what is left of us will be enough
to take upon our shoulders the enormous sum of the future
which awaits us
as after a long voyage.

Translated by Christina Shantz

INCOGNITA

What am I doing hanging from that wing in the shadows?

I confess I'm surprised by this metaphysical flight,
trapped by medusa's eye.
The cities explode like a puddle in the sky
and in mid-life we make ourselves
clots of amazement

Nothing awaits us besides this movement
printed on our hair
and that cataract of smoke between our fingers.

What am I doing here, naked and bleeding
like an angel in the middle of the light?

Translated by Christina Shantz

PABLO PAREDES

BEWARE OF THE MUTT

I liked that her name was Yasna, I like names that advise of poverty, those names like Jhonatan and Jenifer, those names that say beware of the mutt, that mark territory, that tell of the jungle.
The middle class makes jokes about those names, they find them funny and ridiculous, especially anglo deformations that mix with a poor Perez or a poor Carrasco, they laugh and at night they go to the kitsch party at La Blondie. Her name was Yasna and I loved her so. The middle class laughs in function of the names that connote poverty, they intend to mark their difference, their privileges, their idyllic common origin, but the middle class omits last names, they too are Martinez and Hernandez, although preceded by Camilos, Ignacios and Franciscas. They don't go into last names because from there they came. What Deivid [Dayvid] means to the middle class, is the same as Soto for the Upper Class. Her name was Yasna Rivas and I loved her so.

Translated by Scott Graham Meier

THANK YOU FOR DANCING WITH ME

Thank you for dancing with me, for sucking my wound.
These mongoloid arms now don't ask you to say Downs Syndrome.
Thank you for dancing with me who was all wet,
I didn't like that song, but still it was beautiful,
Under the scab it stayed almost the same as before,
Better than before
Because now it's more pink
Some people like to caress scars
And I leave myself alone

I stay still and quiet
So still that the hand no longer sees me
And I stay alone,
More alone than a finger on the hand
Of someone who's cut off four.

Thank you for dancing with me
and telling me
princess, its 12 and you're still so beautiful
because I know I'm ugly,
that my size is disgusting
that I have written in my stained skin
the trip that great grandmother took from Neuquén to Chile
that I have written like an infection in the pores
father's prison,
that's why I thank you for dancing with me
that I write pretty,
but I have more days told than written,
that I need to pornographize my heart,
that I am cracked and spewing
that I splash
that I go on talking of miseries
that I'm drunker than shit
and I become annoying
rarely affectionate
affectionate means horny,
thank you for dancing with me,
for touching my back stained with adolescence
for talking in my ear
for licking me
because I've rested in that lick all of these days,
that lick I'll have for a long time,
because it turns out that tomorrow instead of looking for love in a corner,

instead of going on varnishing my gaucho heart,
I'm going to speak of you,
the only thing I'll change will be the song,
I'm going to say the song was Close to me by the Cure
and that the lick wasn't on the ear but on my sex.

Thank you for dancing with me, for sucking my wound,
for evading any posterity
for taking me
for those rhythms that I don't feel or understand,
I was born in 1982
in those years it seems nobody was dancing,
it seems I was alone for eight years
moving my little foot
in a crib that belonged to another,
thank you for dancing with me
that my body is horrible,
like a physical map of Chile.

Translated by Scott Graham Meier

CONTRIBUTOR BIOGRAPHIES

María Teresa Borys was born in Poland and spent her formative years in Mexico. She earned a Masters degree in Spanish-English Translation from the University of Ottawa and an MBA (Finance) from McGill University. María writes and translates poetry and prose into English, Spanish and Polish.

Armando Roa, born in Santiago in 1966, is a poet, essayist and translator. His work has been published in different anthologies and magazines in Chile and abroad. He has received Chile's National Book Critics Award and the Pablo Neruda Prize (2002). His publications include: *Cartas a la Juventud* (1993); *La Invención de Chile* (1994), an anthology with Jorge Teillier; *El Hombre de Papel y otros poemas* (1994); *Ezra Pound. Homenaje desde Chile* (1995), essays and translations with Armando Uribe; *El Apocalipsis de las Palabras/La Dicha de Enmudecer* (1998-2002); *Elogio de la Melancolía* (1999), essay; "El Navegante" (1999), translation; *Para no morir tan despacio* (1999), narrations; *Ezra Pound. Poesía Temprana* (2000), translation; *Zarabanda de la Muerte Oscura* (2000); *El Mito y la Sombra* (2001), novel; *Robert Browning. Poesía Escogida* (2001), translation; *Estancias en Homenaje a Gregorio Samsa* (2001); *Macbeth, from William Shakespeare* (2002), translation; *Lecturas Anglosajonas* (2002), translation; *Fundación Mítica del Reino de Chile* (2002); *This be the verse* (2003), translation with Marcelo Ríoseco and Diana Dunkelberger.

Armando Uribe, born in 1933, is a writer, poet and lawyer. He studied at Saint George's College—a prestigious English school in Santiago— and law at the Universidad de Chile, where he also later taught. He worked as a diplomat and went to exile in France when Pinochet came to power in 1973. He returned to Chile in 1990. He is a member in various capacities of the Academia Chilena de la Lengua and the Real Academia Española. Part of the 1950s generation, he published his first book of poems, *El transeúnte pálido*, in 1954. His numerous published works include the poetry books *Transeúnte pálido* (1954); *El engañoso laúd* (1956), *No hay lugar* (1970), *Pound* (1963), *Por ser vos quien sois* (1989), *Las críticas de Chile* (1999) and *El fantasma de la sinrazón y El secreto de la poesía* (2001). He has also published works of politics, fiction, religion and law. In 2002 he was awarded the prestigious Altazor Prize in the categories of poetry and essay. He won the Chilean National Prize for Literature in 2004.

Ximena Troncoso, born in Santiago in 1967, is a poet and cultural activist. She studied law at the Universidad de Chile, as well journalism at the Universidad ARSIS. She belongs to the theater and poetry group Anemix, whose performances combine poetry, music and acting to disseminate the works of the great Chilean poets. She has participated in numerous literary workshops, poetry readings and writers conferences at universities, regionally and nationally. Her poems appear in anthologies, magazines and on CD. She forms part of the Press and Cultural Divulgation Department of the Chilean Society of Writers. Her first book, *Frágil*, was published in 2008 by Mago Editores, a Chilean publishing house specializing in young and emerging poets.

Gonzalo Rojas, born in southern Chile in 1917, is a poet, former editor and professor. He studied at the Universidad de Chile, edited the magazine *Antarctica* in Santiago and taught in Valparaiso. From 1938 to 1941, he participated in the surrealist group Mandrágora founded by Braulio Arenas, Teófilo Cid and Enrique Gómez Correa, with avant-garde poets Vicente Huidobro, Fernando Onfray, Gustavo Osorio, Pablo de Rokha and Ludwig Zeller, but soon renounced the avant-garde. Exiled in 1973, he worked at the University of Rostock in East Germany and returned to Chile in 1979, thanks to a Guggenheim scholarship. He has also taught at universities in the United States, Mexico and Spain. In 1992, he was awarded the Queen Sofia Ibero-American Poetry Prize and in that same year won Chile's National

Prize for Literature. In 2003, he was awarded the prestigious Cervantes Prize. His first volume of poems was published in 1948, and his works include: *La miseria del hombre* (1948); *Contra la muerte* (1964); *Oscuro* (1977); *Transtierro* (1979); *Del relámpago* (1981); *50 poemas* (1982); *El alumbrado* (1986); *Antología personal* (1988); *Materia de testamento* (1988); *Antología de aire* (1991); *Desocupado lector* (1990); *Las hermosas* (1991); *Zumbido* (1991); *Río turbio* (1996); *América es la casa y otros poemas* (1998); and *Obra selecta* (1999).

Cecilia Palma, born in Santiago in 1962, belongs to the so-called NN generation of writers who began their craft in 1980s Chile, under the dictatorship. She was on the Board of Directors for the Chilean Society of Writers. Her texts have been translated into Italian, English, Ukrainian, German, French and Norwegian. She has appeared in several anthologies and has received distinctions and grants for her poetic work. Her books include: *Asirme de tus hombros* (2002); *Piano Bar* (2007); *Subway Ediciones* (Bicentenary Prize); *Central Los Molles* (2009); *Vuelvo de Siberia esta tarde* (unpublished – honorary mention in the Eduardo Anguita National Poetry Contest); *El Beso de Judas* (unpublished).

Elías Letelier, born in 1957, belongs to the NN generation of poets who began writing under Pinochet's dictatorship. During that time, he worked extensively in cultural resistance and was imprisoned by the regime. He arrived in Canada in 1981. His books of poetry, published in Spanish, English and French, include: *Mural*, 2003; *Poemas Escogidos*; *Histoire de la Nuit* (1999); *Silence* (1996); *Symphony* (1988); and *Canciones del Gato* (1976). He has published Spanish translations of *Veranda* by the American poet Ken Norris (2004) and *Palabras Sobrevivientes* by Canadian poet Endre Farkas (2003). He is the editor of the anthology *Anaconda. Antología de Poetas Americanos*, translated from the Spanish by Lizabeta Lazañi (2003). He created www.poetas.com, a pioneer in cyber poetry in the Americas, and is the director of the publishing house Poetas Antiimperialistas de América.

Clemente Riedemann joined the Marxist Revolutionary Left Movement (MIR) in high school. As a university student in 1973, he was detained as a political prisoner until 1974. He worked as a creative writer and cultural activist for civil rights in Chile, in poetry and in popular song with the duet Schwenke y Nilo in the 1980s. He has published theater, poetry and cultural criticism. He has appeared in almost all relevant anthologies of Chilean poetry in that country and abroad since 1985. His work has been translated into English and German. In 1990, he won the prestigious Pablo Neruda Prize for Poetry. His books include: *Rito de Pasaje* (2000), poetry and artwork; *Karra Maw'n y otros poemas* (1995); *El Viaje* (1990), chronicles; *Primer Arqueo* (1989), poetry; *Hacia la casa de ninguna parte* (1981), poetry.

Omar Cid, born in Talca in 1967, is an educational psychologist who has studied law at the Universidad Finis Terrae in Santiago. He was published in the poetry anthology *Travesía por el río de las nieblas* (2000). In June 2008, was included in the *Antología de poesía y narrativa chilena* by the publisher MAGO Editores. In November 2008, he participated in the anthology *Río Bellavista*. He is co-author of *PURO Chile, Suciedad democrática*, a book of articles about contemporary Chilean culture and society. Some of his poems were selected for the anthology of French Hispanic poetry *Arcoiris* (2008). He is cultural editor of the Chilean virtual newspaper *Crónica Digital* and collaborates with various Chilean virtual media, such as *Diario Clarín* and *Chile Informa*.

Luis Lama was born in the province of Talcahuano. He studied politics and philosophy at the Pontificia Universidad Católica de Chile in Santiago. He taught philosophy at the Universidad de Antofagasta until 1973. He received a Masters degree in Comparative Literature from Carleton University in Ottawa (Canada). His work has appeared in literary magazines, periodicals and anthologies, such as *Anthos, Canadian Fiction Magazine, White Wall Review, Arc, Indigo, Zymergy, Quarry, Books in Canada, Libido, Alter Vox, Boreal* (an anthology of Hispanic-Canadian poets), *Symbiosis* (an anthology of Hispanic-Canadian poets), and *Northern Cronopios* (an anthology of Chilean prose writers in Canada). In 1989, Split Quotation published his first collection of prose poetry *The History Teacher in Ecstasy*. He was a finalist for the Archibald Lampman Award. *Cassandra or the Seven Doors* was published in 1991. In 2007, he published *El Diario del Gato Negro* and *Alien Land*.

Leo Lobos, born in Santiago de Chile in 1966, is a poet, essayist, translator and visual artist. Winner of the UNESCO-Aschberg Literature Prize in 2002, he was granted a creative residency period at the Centre d'Art Marnay in Marnay-sur-Seine, France. He exhibited and was resident artist at the Jardim das Artes research centre in Cerquillo, São Paulo, Brazil. His published works include: *Cartas de más abajo* (1992); *+Poesía* (1995); *Perdidos en La Habana y otros poemas* (1996); *Ángeles eléctricos* (1997); *Camino a Copa de Oro* (1998); *Turbosílabas. Poesía Reunida 1986-2003* (2003); *Un sin nombre* (2005); *Nieve* (2006); *Vía Regia* (2007); *No permitas que el paisaje esté triste* (2007). He has published and read texts on art and literature in Chile, Argentina, Peru, Brazil, Cuba, the United States, Mexico, Spain, Portugal, France and Germany. He has translated several Brazilian poets from Portuguese into Spanish. His art work is in private and public collections in Chile, Mexico, the United States, Brazil and France.

Claudio Durán, born in 1939, was exiled to Canada following the military coup that deposed the government of President Salvador Allende on September 11, 1973. In 1974, he became a Professor of Philosophy and Social Science at York University in Toronto, where he remains a Senior Scholar. He has published the following books of poetry: *Homenaje*(1980); *After the Usual Clients Have Gone Home* (1982); *Después del Silencio/After Silence*, with Chilean poet Jaime Gómez Rogers (1986); *Santiago* (1988); *La infancia y los exilios* (2006), also published in Canada in a bilingual edition. His poetry has appeared in several anthologies, such as *Chilean Literature in*

Canada (1982), and he has organized poetry readings in Toronto. His most important research has focused on the discourse of the Chilean newspaper *El Mercurio*, a traditionally right-wing publication.

Nieves Fuenzalida (1938) is a former teacher of philosophy from Santiago. A winner of a poetry contest jointly organized by Carleton University and the University of Ottawa. His book *Three of Us Remain* was published in Ottawa in 1988, the *39avos fragmentos del Clan: Acerca de 4 Álamos -1 Álamo= 3 Álamos* was published in the 1990 in Chile. She has published in *Antología de la poesía femenina latinoamericana en Canada* (1992) and *Symbiosis: An Intercultural Anthology Of Poetry, Boreal, Antología de poesía latinoamericana en Canadá* (1992); The Chilean-Canadian Poetry issue of the magazine Arc (1995), and numerous virtual and printed literary magazines. Nieves spent a year at the notorious "3 Álamos" concentration camp in Chile in 1974. She has lived in Canada since 1975.

Luciano P. Díaz, born in Santiago de Chile, has lived in Canada since 1978. His books include *The Stops Of A Phantom Train* (1990) and *The Thin Man And Me* (1994), the Spanish version of which was published in 2008 as *El Flaco y yo*. He edited *Symbiosis: An Intercultural Anthology Of Poetry* (1992) and *Symbiosis In Prose: An Anthology Of Short Fiction* (1995). In 1995, he was guest editor of ARC, a Canadian poetry magazine, on an issue dedicated to Chilean Canadian poetry. He has participated in various international poetry symposiums and festivals in Mexico, Toronto, Boston, Montreal, Vancouver, Ottawa, Kingston, Quebec, North Carolina and elsewhere, and is the co-author of the anthology by ten Chilean Canadian poets, *El lugar de la memoria* (2009). His work has appeared in various anthologies. He was a co-founder of the El Dorado cultural workshop and is co-editor of the multilingual literary magazine *Alter Vox*. He directs the small publishing house Verbum Veritas.

Rodrigo Lira was born in Santiago de Chile in 1949. He studied psychology, philosophy and arts at the Universidad de Chile. During Salvador Allende's government, he worked at the publishing house Quimantú. Most of his writing was produced between 1977 and 1981. In 1979, he won first prize in the poetry contest sponsored by the magazine *La Bicicleta*. He committed suicide in 1981, at the age of 32, and became a mythical figure of the Chilean neo avant-garde. The anthology *Proyecto de obras completas* was published posthumously in 1984. Another book of poems is *Declaración jurada*, a compilation of six texts not published in the first anthology. He is considered a key author of his generation.

José Ángel Cuevas started to write poetry in the late 1960s, as a member of the Grupo América in Santiago. In 1979, he published *Efectos personales y Dominios públicos*. This was followed by other books: *Introducción a Santiago* (1982); *Contravidas* (1983); *Canciones rock para chilenos* (1987); *Cánticos amorosos y patrióticos* (1988); *Adiós muchedumbres* (1989); *30 poemas del ex poeta José Ángel Cuevas* (1992) and others. He studied philosophy at the Universidad de Chile. His work has been widely published and translated, being one of the most important names in contemporary Chilean poetry and a chronicler of Santiago life for the last four decades.

Sergio Badilla Castro was born in Valparaíso in 1947. During his exile in Sweden, he participated in the Grupo Taller and Pelican Group of Arts, with the Uruguayan poet Roberto Mascaró and the Chilean visual artist Juan Castillo. At the time, he was also director of the publishing house Bikupa, a journalist with Radio Suecia International and an anthropologist at the University of Stockholm. He teaches at the Universidad La República in Santiago de Chile. He has published the short stories *Más abajo de mi rama* (1980) and the books of poetry *La morada del signo* (1982); *Cantonírico* (1983); *Reverberaciones de piedras acuáticas* (1985); *Terrenalis* (1989); *Saga nórdica* (1996); and *La mirada temerosa del bastardo* (2004).

Jaime Gómez Rogers (1940-2005) was a poet considered to be an emblematic figure of the 1960s generation. He studied Spanish at the Pedagogical Institute at the Universidad de Chile, where he was part of the Spanish Department's literary academy, Academia Literaria . His books of poetry are: *Deshojándome* (1962); *El circo* (1971); *El jardín de las palabras* (1976); *Signos* (1978); *Imágenes* (1979); *Tierra madre* (1980); *El corazón enterrado* (1985); *El Tabo* (1985); *Carta a un poeta* (1985); *Diccionario cabal* (1986); *Adiós a la ciudad* (1989); *Entonces vino el mar* (1989); *Canto al amor* (1990); *El huerto en la montaña* (1990); *El ángel de la orilla* (1991); *Entre el silencio y la llovía* (1999); *Por amor* (2000); *Desde la orilla* (2001); *Piedra del trueno* (2002); and *Bitácora* (2003).

José María Memet, born 1957, is a poet, cultural activist and editor. His writing developed under the dictatorship of Augusto Pinochet, being of the so called NN generation. He has published numerous books of poems, including: *Poemas crucificados* (1977); *Bajo amenaza* (1979); *Cualquiera de nosotros* (1980); *Los gestos de otra vida* (1985); *Canto de gallos al amanecer* (1986); *La casa de la ficción y otros poemas* (1988); *El duelo* (1994); *Un animal noble y hermoso cercado entre ballestas* (1995); and *Amanecer sin Dioses* (1999). He has been awarded thirty-nine national acknowledgments, include the Gabriela Mistral (1977) and Pablo Neruda (1996) prizes. Founder and General Director of ChilePoesía, which organizes the Encuentro Internacional de Poetas, the Universidad de la Poesía, and the prizes "Armando Rubio Huidobro para Poetas Jóvenes" and "Chilectra, Ilumina tu Imaginación". He has read poems and papers and participated in poetry festivals, book fairs and other international poetic and cultural events in more than thirty countries.

Waldo Rojas was born in Concepción in 1944, and went to university in Santiago. He has lived in Paris since 1974, where he teaches at the University of Paris I (Sorbonne) in the Department of Contemporary History. In the 1960s, he published in magazines and was linked to different Chilean poetic groups of that era, such as Trilce, Arúspice, Tebaida, and is considered one of the most important poets of his generation. His poems have been published in numerous literary magazines, translated into various languages and featured in numerous anthologies in Chile and abroad. His books of poetry include: *Agua removida* (1964); *Pájaro en tierra* (1966); *Príncipe de Naipes* (1966); *Cielorraso* (1971); *El Puente Oculto* (1981); *Chiffré à la Villa d'Hadrien (Cifrado en la Villa Adriana)* (1984); *Almenara* (1985); *Deriva florentina* (1989 and 1993); *Fuente Itálica* (1991); *Cuatro poemas, Cuatro grabados*, with artwork by Guido Llinas (1999). An anthology of his poetry entitled *Poesía Continua (Antología 1965-1992)* was published in 1995.

Alfredo Lavergne was born in Valparaíso in 1951. He moved to Québec (Canada) in 1975, and returned to Chile in 2005. His work has been included in anthologies and magazines. His books of poetry published in Montreal include: *Cahier Fluvial* (1997); *El Puente* (1995); *La mano en la velocidad* (1993); *Alguien soñó que no moría / On ne rêve pas encore à la mort* (1993); *El viejo de los zapatos* (1991); *Retro-perspectiva / Retro-perspective* (1991); *Palos con palitos* (1990); *Rasgos separados / Traits distinctifs* (1989); *Índice agresivo* (1987); *Alas dispersas* (1986). He appears in *Compañeros, Anthology of Writings about Latin America in Canada* (1990); *Enjambre, Poesía latinoamericana en el Québec* (1990); *Odes, Dreams, and Diaspora, Poesía Chileno-Canadiense*, special issue of ARC magazine (1995); *Boreal: Antología de Poesía Latinoamericana en Canadá* (2002); *Antología de poetas Americanos. Canto a un prisionero* (2005); and *Critical Study of Ten Latin American Writers of Canada*.

Erik Martínez was born in Santiago. He studied in the Spanish Department of Pedagogical Institute of at the Universidad de Chile. In 1974, he emigrated to Canada and obtained a Masters degree in Spanish from Queen's University (Kingston). He taught literature and translation at Queen's and at the Universities of Western Ontario and Ottawa. In Chile, he was a member of the School of Santiago avant-garde poetry group. Together with other exiled Chilean writers

(Leandro Urbina, Gonzalo Millán, Jorge Etcheverry, Naín Nómez and Ramón Sepúlveda), he founded Ediciones Cordillera, a Chilean publishing house in Canada, where he published *Tequila Sunrise* in 1985. His poems have appeared in different anthologies and magazines in Chile, Canada, Germany and other countries. He has presented papers on literary criticism at various academic institutions in Canada and United States

Gonzalo Millán (1947-2006) studied literature at the Universidad de Concepción and the Universidad de Chile, and belonged to the Spanish Department's Literary Academy at the Pedagogical Institute, and formed part of Arúspice, a poetry group from the 1960s. He lived in Canada, where he co-founded the publishing house Ediciones Cordillera, which published his book *La ciudad* and the anthologies *Vida* and *Strange Houses*. He did visual poetry and had solo exhibits in Chile, Canada, the United States and Holland. He was awarded important distinctions, such as the Pedro de Oña Prize (1968), the Pablo Neruda Prize (1987) and the Altazor Prize (2006) for his book *Autorretrato de memoria*. His books include: *La Ciudad* (1979, with other editions in 1994 and 2007); *Vida* (1984); *Seudónimos de la muerte* (1984); *Virus* (1987); *Dragón que se muerde la cola* (1987); *5 poemas eróticos* (1990); *Strange houses*, an anthology of his complete works in English (1991); *Trece lunas* (1997); *Claroscuro* (2002); *Autorretrato de memoria* (2005); *Veneno de escorpión azul. Diario de Vida y de Muerte* (2007) and *Gabinete de papel* (2008). He is considered one of the most important names in the landscape of contemporary Chilean poetry.

Naín Nómez was a member of the School of Santiago, an avant-garde Chilean poetry group from the 1960s, together with Jorge Etcheverry, Erik Martínez and Julio Piñones, with whom he was the co-editor of *33 nombres claves de la actual poesía chilena* (1968), a controversial anthology that favored the avant-garde tradition and presence in Chilean poetry. He is Professor of Chilean and Latin American Literature at the Universidad de Santiago in Chile. He has also taught at the University of Toronto (Canada), Queen's University (Kingston, Canada) and California State University (Long Beach, USA). Nómez is the author of several books on Chilean poets, including Pablo de Rokha and Pablo Neruda, and has published a number of volumes of his own poetry, including *Historias del reino vigilado/Stories of a Guarded Kingdom* (1981), *Burning Bridges* (1987) and *El Fuego va Borrando* (1989). He has published his poetry and criticism extensively, and has read poetry and papers at numerous international events and venues. His work includes the *Antología Critica de la Poesía Chilena* in several volumes, an ongoing work, a poetry anthology commented and contextualized – perhaps the most ambitious project of its kind ever undertaken in Chile.

Rosamel del Valle, a pseudonym for Moisés Filadelfio Gutiérrez Gutiérrez (1900-1965), was one of the foremost surrealist Chilean poets. He went to Santiago in 1918 and worked as linotypist, publishing poems under different pseudonyms, until his first book *Los poemas lunados* (1920) used the pseudonym Rosamel del Valle for the first time. He met another of the most important surrealist Chilean poets, Humberto Díaz Casanueva in 1923. He lived in New York where he worked freelance for the UN. Rosamel del Valle is a fundamental poet of the Chilean poetic avant-garde and some critics compare him to Vicente Huidobro, Pablo Neruda and Pablo de Rokha. His books include: *Los poemas lunados* (1920); Mirador (1926); *País blanco y negro* (1929); *Poesía* (1939); *Orfeo* (1944); *El joven olvido* (1949); *Fuegos y ceremonias* (1952); *La visión comunicable* (1956); *El corazón escrito* (1960); *Adiós enigma tornasol* (posthumous publication in 1965); and the poetic prose volume *El sol es un pájaro cautivo en el reloj*; (1963). He also wrote short stories, novels and essays, such as *La violencia creadora, La Poesía de Humberto Díaz-Casanueva* (1959) and other works.

Vicente Huidobro was born Vicente García Huidobro Fernández in Santiago in 1893, and he died in 1948. One of the foremost avant-garde poets of the Spanish language and creator of Creacionismo, he is one of the five most relevant poets of Chile, along with Pablo Neruda, Gabriela Mistral, Pablo de Rokha and Nicanor Parra. In his case, as with the other poets mentioned, his main accomplishment was the renewal of and experimentation with poetic language. He was well known in Europe, particularly in Paris. He did much to introduce his countrymen to contemporary European innovations in poetics. He went to Paris in 1916, after publishing poetry in Chile. He collaborated with Guillaume Apollinaire and Pierre Reverdy on the literary magazine *Nord-Sud*. He exemplified "creationism" in *Poemas árticos* (1918) and *Saisons choisies* (1921). In 1918, in Madrid, he was enthusiastically received in avant-garde circles and was one of the founders of Ultraísmo. Traveling frequently between Europe and Chile, he was largely responsible for creating the climate of literary experimentation, based on French models, that prevailed in post-World War I Chile. He accomplished this as much through his well-publicized exploits (such as his semiserious candidacy for the presidency of Chile) as through his frequent magazine articles and poetry. He wrote "creationist" novels like *Sátiro o el poder de las palabras* (1939). His book of poetry *Altazor*, written between 1919 and 1931, is one of the most important books of poetry in the Spanish language.

Pablo de Rokha was a pseudonym for Pablo Díaz Loyola, considered one of the five great Chilean poets, along with Gabriela Mistral, Pablo Neruda, Vicente Huidobro and Nicanor Parra. Like them, he was an innovator of poetic language, a poet who combined the avant-garde approach to poetry with an axiological humanistic meaning. He won the Chilean National Prize for Literature in 1965. As a child, he lived on a farm in southern Chile and studied in Talca. He moved to Santiago in 1911. In 1916, he married the poet Luisa Anabalón Sanderson, who wrote under the pseudonym Winétt de Rokha. He wrote for different newspapers and published his first poems. He worked with the Frente Popular political party that elected Pedro Aguirre Cerda in 1938. In 1994, then President Juan Antonio Ríos named him cultural ambassador of Chile to America. As a leftist, he maintained a bitter rivalry with Pablo

Neruda, also a communist. He committed suicide in 1968. His works include: *Oda a la memoria de Máximo Gorki* (1936); *Moisés* (1937); *Pablo de Rokha Gran temperatura* (1937); *Cinco cantos rojos* (1938); *Morfología del espanto* (1942); *Canto al ejército rojo* (1944); *Poemas continentales* (1945); *América: los cinco estilos del Pacífico* (1948); *Arenga sobre el arte* (1949); *Carta Magna del continente* (1949); *Fusiles de sangre* (1950); *Funeral por los héroes y los mártires de Corea* (1950); *Fuego negro* (1953); *Arte grande o ejercicio del realismo* (1953); *Antología* (1954); *Neruda y yo* (1955); *Idioma del mundo* (1958); *Genio del pueblo* (1960); *Acera e invierno* (1961); *Canto de fuego a China Popular* (1963); *China Roja*, (1964); *Estilo de masas* (1965) *Mundo a mundo: Francia*; (1967); and *El amigo Piedra* (posthumous, 1989)

Julio Miralles was born in 1971 and died in 2008. A poet from northern Chile, he initially lived in Vicuña, where he stared to write. His first book, *De Astros y Confabulaciones*, was published in Canada in 1992. In Vicuña, he was awarded the Gabriela Mistral award for outstanding citizens in 1994. That same year he was awarded first prize in the short story contest sponsored by the Huasco Museum. He then participated in numerous poetry readings, book fairs and at the Universidad de la Serena. In 1995, he won first prize in a contest for best letter to one's father and was then decorated for his poetic work by the city of Vicuña in 1996. In 1997, he moved to Iquique, where he wrote the play *De cómo me hice sombra*. At the Universidad Arturo Pratt, he led the literary workshop *Antawara* and in 1999 published *Las fórmulas secretas de la soledad*. His other books of poetry, primarily in virtual format include: *Marea y necesidades* (1993); *Lacrimario Estremecido* (1995); *Fragmentos del Tatuado* (1997); *De Cómo me hice Sombra* (1998); *Los Ángeles Prohibidos por el Amanecer* (2005) and *City Tour* (2007).

Jorge Etcheverry, born in 1945, is a former member of the School of Santiago and Grupo América from the 1960s. He lives in Canada and has published poetry, prose, criticism and various articles in several countries. His books of poetry are: *The Escape Artist* (1981); *La Calle* (1986); *The Witch* (1986); *Tánger* (1991); *A Vuelo de Pájaro* (1998); *Vitral con Pájaros*,(2004); and *Reflexión Hacia el Sur* (2004). Lately, he has appeared in anthologies such as *Cien microcuentos chilenos* (2002); *Los poetas y el general* (2002); *Anaconda, Antología di Poeti Americani* (2003); *El lugar de la memoria. Poetas y narradores de Chile* (2007); *Latinocanadá* (2007); *Poéticas de Chile. Chilean Poets* (2007); *100 cuentos breves de todo el mundo* (2007); and *The Changing Faces of Chilean Poetry: A Translation of Avant Garde, Women's, and Protest Poetry* (2008).

Gabriela Mistral (1889-1957), pseudonym for Lucila Godoy y Alcayaga, was born in Vicuña, Chile. The daughter of a dilettante poet, she began to write poetry as a village schoolteacher after a passionate romance with a railway employee who committed suicide. She taught elementary and secondary school for many years until her poetry made her famous. She played an important role in the educational systems of Mexico and Chile, was active in cultural committees of the League of Nations, and was Chilean consul in Naples, Madrid, and Lisbon. She held honorary degrees from the Universities of Florence and Guatemala and was an honorary member of various cultural societies in Chile as well as in the United States, Spain, and Cuba. She taught Spanish literature in the United States at Columbia University, Middlebury College, Vassar College, and at the University of Puerto Rico.

The love poems in memory of the dead, *Sonetos de la muerte* (1914), made her known throughout Latin America, but her first great collection of poems, *Desolación [Despair]*, was not published until 1922. In 1924 appeared *Ternura [Tenderness]*, a volume of poetry dominated by the theme of childhood; the same theme, linked with that of maternity, plays a significant role in Tala, poems published in 1938. Her complete poetry was published in 1958.

Víctor Lidio Jara Martínez (September 28, 1932 – September 15, 1973[1]) was a Chilean teacher, theatre director, poet, singer-songwriter, political activist and member of the Communist Party of Chile. A distinguished theatre director, he devoted himself to the development of Chilean theatre, directing a broad array of works from locally produced Chilean plays, to the classics of the world stage, to the experimental work of Ann Jellicoe. Simultaneously he developed in the field of music and played a pivotal role among neo-folkloric artists who established the Nueva Canción Chilena (New Chilean Song) movement which led to a revolution in the popular music of his country under the Salvador Allende government. Shortly after the Chilean coup of 11 September 1973, he was arrested, tortured and ultimately shot to death with 44 bullet shots by machine gun fire. His body was later thrown out into the street of a shanty town in Santiago.[2] The contrast between the themes of his songs, on love, peace and social justice and the brutal way in which he was murdered transformed Jara into a symbol of struggle for human rights and justice across Latin America.

Enrique Lihn Carrasco (3 September 1929 – 10 July 1988) was a Chilean poet, playwright, and novelist. The son of Enrique Lihn Doll and María Carrasco Délano, he married Ivette Mingram (1932-2008) and they had one daughter: Andrea María Lihn Mingram, an actress.

Born in 1929 at Santiago, Chile, Lihn aspired to be a painter but after a failed attempt during university, he abandoned that dream to pursue writing. Lihn proceeded to develop into a poet, playwright, and novelist. He taught literature at the University of Chile. Lihn views both the past and the future as forms of death, and his emphasis on this point is evident throughout his literary works. His work revolved around his contempt for the contemporary dictatorship, as Chile was governed by a military junta. Works layered with social, political, and religious commentary are common throughout Lihn's canon. His final book, *Diario de Muerte* was written in the six weeks preceding his death from cancer in Santiago, and the evening before he died, he corrected the proofs.

Nicanor Parra Sandoval (born September 5, 1914) is a mathematician and poet born in San Fabián de Alico, Chile, who has been considered to be a popular poet in Chile with enormous influence and popularity in Latin America.[1] He describes himself as an "anti-poet," due to his distaste for standard poetic pomp and function—after recitations he would exclaim Me retracto de todo lo dicho, or, "I take back everything I said".Trying to get away from the conventions of poetry, Parra's poetic language renounces the refinement of most Latin American literature and adopts a more colloquial tone. His first collection, "Poemas y Antipoemas" (1954) is a classic of Latin American literature, one of the most influential Spanish poetry collections of the twentieth century. Nicanor Parra was born in 1914 near Chillán, a city in southern Chile, the son of a schoolteacher. In 1933, he entered the Instituto Pedagógico of the University of Chile, and qualified as a teacher of mathematics and physics in 1938, one year after his first book appeared: *Cancionero sin Nombre*. After teaching in Chilean secondary schools, he went in 1943 to Brown University in the U.S. to continue his studies in physics and then he went in 1948 to Oxford in England to study cosmology. He returned to Chile as professor at the University in 1946. Since 1952, Parra has been professor of theoretical physics in Santiago and has read his poetry in England, France, Russia, Mexico, Cuba, and the United States. He has published several books.

Pablo Neruda (July 12, 1904 – September 23, 1973) was the pen name and, later, legal name of the Chilean poet and politician Neftalí Ricardo Reyes Basoalto. He chose his pen name after Czech poet Jan Neruda. Neruda wrote in a variety of styles such as erotically charged love poems as in his collection *Twenty Poems of Love and a Song of Despair*, surrealist poems, historical epics, and overtly political manifestos. In 1971 Neruda won the Nobel Prize for Literature. Colombian novelist Gabriel García Marquez once called him "the greatest poet of the 20th century in any language." Neruda always wrote in green ink as it was the color of (hope). On July 15, 1945, at

Pacaembu Stadium in São Paulo, Brazil, he read to 100,000 people in honor of Communist revolutionary leader Luís Carlos Prestes. During his lifetime, Neruda occupied many diplomatic posts and served a stint as a senator for the Chilean Communist Party. When a Conservative Chilean President González Videla outlawed communism in Chile in 1948, a warrant was issued for Neruda's arrest. Friends hid him for months in a house basement in the Chilean port of Valparaíso. Later, Neruda escaped into exile through a mountain pass near Maihue Lake into Argentina. Years later, Neruda was a close collaborator to socialist President Salvador Allende. When Neruda returned to Chile after his Nobel Prize acceptance speech, Allende invited him to read at the Estadio Nacional before 70,000 people. Neruda was hospitalized with cancer at the time of the Chilean coup d'état led by Augusto Pinochet. Three days after being hospitalized, Neruda died of heart failure. Already a legend in life, Neruda's death reverberated around the world. Pinochet had denied permission to transform Neruda's funeral into a public event. However, thousands of grieving Chileans disobeyed the curfew and crowded the streets.

Óscar Arturo Hahn Garcés (born 1938 in Iquique, Chile) is a Chilean writer and poet. Known in Chile as one of the writers of the Generation of the 70s (also known as the "Dispersed" or "Decimated Generation" - "Generacion Trilce"), Hahn studied at the Pedagogical Institute of Santiago during his youth. His first steps in poetry can be traced back to his adolescence in Rancagua.

In 1959 he won the Student Federation of Chile's Prize in Poetry. In the year 1961 he won the Society of Chilean Writers' Alerce Prize for the work *This Black Rose (Esta Rosa Negra)*. In 1967 he won the Unique Prize of the First Contest in Northern Poetry of the University of Chile for the (then) regional seat of Antofagasta.[6]

Hahn left Chile in 1974 to set down new roots in the USA. He was awarded the degree of Doctor of Philosophy by the University of Maryland College Park, and between 1978 and 1988 he collaborated in the composition of the Handbook of Latin American Studies issued by the Library of Congress, Washington, D.C. He is a member of the Chilean Academy of Language, and sat on the organizing committee for the Comités del V Congreso Internacional de la Lengua Española (CILE).

Hahn won the Society of Chilean Writers' Alerce Prize, the Municipal Prize of Santiago, and the Altazor Prize (2003). He has taught Latin American literature at the University of Iowa.

Raúl Zurita was born in Santiago, Chile in 1950. He started out studying engineering before turning to poetry. His early work is a ferocious response to Augusto Pinochet's 1973 military coup. Like many other Chileans, Zurita was arrested and tortured. When he was released, he helped to form a radical artistic group CADA, and he became renowned for his provocative and intensely physical public performances. He has written what are perhaps the most massively scaled poems ever created. He has done this with earth-moving equipment and with smoke-trailing aircraft. In the early 1980s, Zurita famously sky-wrote passages from his poem, "The New Life," over New York and later—still during the reign of Pinochet—he bulldozed the phrase "Ni Pena Ni Miedo" ("Without Pain Or Fear") into the Atacama Desert which, for its length, can only be seen from the sky.*
An article in *Jacket Magazine* elucidates, "He says that in those days of brutality and distrust and terror...he began to imagine writing poems in the sky, on the faces of cliffs, in the desert.... He started to imagine that he might fight sadistic force with poems as insubstantial as contrails in the air over a city." Zurita's renowned poetic trilogy, composed over a span of 15 years, is considered one of the singular poetic achievements in Latin American poetry: *Purgatory* appeared in 1979, *Anteparadise* in 1982, and *The New Life* in 1993.

Zurita is the recipient of numerous awards, including a Guggenheim Fellowship, the Casa de las Americas Prize from Cuba and the National Poetry Prize of Chile. His work has been translated into a dozen languages. In English, *INRI* is translated by William Rowe and published by Marick Press. *Purgatory*, translated by Anna Deeny, is forthcoming from The University of California Press. Zurita's other poetry collections include: *El Paraíso Esta Vacío, Canto a Su Amor, Desaparecido, El Amor de Chile, Los Países muertos, In Memoriam, Las Ciudades de Agua.* He has just completed a book that includes "Inscriptions Facing the Sea," a project to inscribe 22 phrases in the cliffs of the north coast of Chile that would only be read from the sea.

Marjorie Agosín (born June 15, 1955) is an award-winning poet, essayist, fiction writer, activist, and professor. She is a prolific author: her published books, including those she has written as well as those she has edited, number over eighty. Her two most recent books are both poetry collections, *The Light of Desire / La Luz del Deseo*, translated by Lori Marie Carlson (Swan Isle Press, 2009), and *Secrets in the Sand: The Young Women of Juárez*, translated by Celeste Kostopulos-Cooperman (White Pine Press, 2006), about the female homicides in Ciudad Juárez. She teaches Spanish language and Latin American literature at Wellesley College. She has won notability for her outspokenness for women rights in Chile. The United Nations has honored her for her work on human rights. She also won many important literary awards. The Chilean government awarded her with the Gabriela Mistral Medal of Honor for Life Achievement in 2002. Agosín was born in 1955 to Moises and Frida Agosín in Chile, where she lived her childhood in a German community.

Elicura Chihuailaf Nahuelpán (1952 in Quechurehue, Cautín Province) is a Mapuche Chilean poet and author whose works are written both in Mapudungun and in Spanish, and have been translated into many other languages as well. He has also translated the works of other poets, such as Pablo Neruda, into Mapudungun.

He has been referred to as the lonco, or chieftain, of Mapudungun poetry, and works at recording and preserving the oral tradition of his people. "Elicura" is from the Mapudungun phrase for "transparent stone", "Chihuailaf" means "fog spread on the lake", and "Nahuelpán" is "tiger/cougar".

In his book *Recado Confidencial a los Chilenos*, he talks about a childhood around the bonfire, in which he learnt the art of conversation ("nvtram") and the advice of the elderly ("gulam"). Similarly, nature with its diversity taught him the cosmic vitality hid from those unwary. This need to express his cultural richness, diverse in itself, made him become an Oralitor, that is, carrier of the oral expression of the Mapuche elderly, this destiny being told by means of "Blue Dreams" (Kallfv Pewma): This will be a singer, you said / giving me the Blue Horse of the Word. In Recado Confidencial a los Chilenos, the poet presents a deeply felt defense of Mother Nature, whom the Mapuche consider threatened by the dominant culture: post-modern capitalism. Considering the current environmental crisis, his message should be listened not only by Chileans but by everybody. The English translation of *Recado Confidencial a los Chilenos (Message to Chileans*; translated by Celso Cambiazo) is now in print published by Trafford Publishing in 2009.

Cecilia Vicuña, who was born in Santiago, Chile, is a poet, filmmaker, painter, installation artist, and sculptor. She studied at the National School of Fine Arts in Santiago and achieved national acclaim as a painter early in her career. Many of the paintings she executed in 1970 and 1971 that depicted political leaders and addressed feminist concerns proved to be highly controversial in Chile. In 1967 Vicuña was a founder of the group Tribu No (the No Tribe), which staged public interventions and circulated manifestos that were inspired in part by the manifestos of the avant-garde groups in Europe and South America in the 1910s and 1920s.

Vicuña had her first solo exhibition in 1971 at the National Museum of Fine Arts in Santiago. She filled the gallery with dry leaves for a work she titled *Otoño (Autumn)* and dedicated to the construction of socialism in Chile. In 1972 Vicuña went to London with a fellowship to study at the Slade School of Fine Arts. She became an exile from her home country when General Augusto Pinochet staged a coup and murdered President Salvador Allende in 1973. Vicuña had been a supporter of Allende's Popular Unity government; after the coup she became an active participant in the Chilean solidarity movement in London. She was one of the founding members of Artists for Democracy, and in 1974 she organized the Arts Festival for Democracy in Chile at the Royal College of Art in London.

In 1977 Vicuña moved to Bogotá, Colombia, where she painted and did street performances and theatrical design. She created a sixteen-millimeter film called *What Is Poetry to You?* (1980), in which she proposes the title's question to prostitutes, beggars, policemen, and passersby and documents their responses. Vicuña traveled throughout the country, performing her poetry and speaking about the political situation in Chile. In 1980 she moved to New York, where she met and married the Argentine painter and writer César Paternosto.

In 1966 Vicuña made the first of her precarios, small sculptures and installations assembled from found objects. Her precarios are, as their name suggests, fragile, often ephemeral, and vulnerable to the contingencies of their environment. The performative aspect of the precarios is as integral to their meanings as the assembled objects or the symbolic resonance of their materials. As Vicuña notes, the Latin root of their name is precis, meaning prayer. In "Entering," published in *QUIPoem*, Vicuña describes the "precarious" as that which is figured through prayer, through acts of offering and desiring. Prayer, for Vicuña, turns on the concept of reciprocity: her artistic process is dialogical, addressed to the manifest qualities of her materials and environments as well as to what remains unseen or potential within them. Vicuña's transitory objects reveal already existing yet unnoticed relationships. Vicuña does not claim authorship of these relationships. Rather, she invests them with meaning and makes them visible, indicating them with her objects and tracing them with the movements of her own body.

Guido Eytel was born in Temuco, in southern Chile. He is a storyteller and poet. He has won several prizes in national short story and poetry, among them the Gabriela Mistral's poetry, and the newspaper La Tercera story.

In 1997 he published his first novel - *Houses at the water* - which won the Premio Municipal de Novela Award and the Academy of the Chilean Academy of Language. In late 1999 he published his second novel, *Blood poured your mouth*.

He studied journalism, construction and education in Castilian. He was then a bookseller, cook, and bookseller. He was a journalist in Argentina (where he lived for three years).

Carmen Berenguer (born in Santiago in 1946) is a Chilean poet and writer.Her poetry has been collected in several anthologies as *Poetry Current Territory (Publisher Little Venice, 1993), Women Poets of Chile (Linda Irene Koski, Editorial Cuarto Propio, 1998), Une Anthology (Henry Deluy, Editions Farrago, 2004) Chilean Poetry Unclassified (1973-1990) (Gonzalo Contreras, 2006) New Poetry Anthology Hispanoamericano (Leo Zelada, compiler, Lord Byron Ediciones, 2005-2006).*

She has been editor of the magazines *Sheet X Eye*, 1984, and *Al Margen*, 1986. In 1987, together with other writers organized the First Congress of Women's Literature.

In October 1989, participates in Stockholm, Sweden in the International Poetry Festival: The reconstruction of the time, organized by Sergio Badilla Castillo poet and writer Sun Axelsson.

In 2003, Congress presented the documentary Crime and Treason (Address of women in politics and in art). His work is not limited to poetry and chronicles, but also extends to the visual and performance art.

It has been translated into English, Swedish, French and Iranian. In 1997 she is benefited by obtaining the Simon Guggenheim Fellowship. In March 2008, gets the Pablo Neruda Ibero-American Prize being awarded for the first time a Chilean woman.

Héctor Hernández Montecinos was born in Santiago, Chile in 1979. His books of poetry that were published between 2001 and 2003 are collected in [guión] (Lom Ediciones: Santiago, Chile, 2008); [coma] (Lom Ediciones, 2009) collects his writings from 2004-2006. His other books include *Putamadre* (Zignos: Lima, 2005), *Ay de Mi* (Ripio:

Santiago, 2006), *La poesia chilena soy yo* (Mandrágora cartonera: Cochabamba, 2007), *Segunda mano* (Zignos: Lima, 2007), *A 1000* (Lustra editores: Lima, 2008), *Livro Universal* (Demonio negro: Sao Paulo, 2008, traducido al portugués), *Poemas para muchachos en llamas* (RdlPS: Ciudad de México, 2008), *La Escalera* (Yerba Mala cartonera: La Paz, 2008) *El secreto de esta estrella* (Felicita cartonera: Asunción, 2008), *La interpretación de mis sueños* (Moda y Pueblo: Stgo, 2008) y *NGC 224* (Literal: Ciudad de México, 2009). He has been invited to present his poetry in Germany, Argentina, Brazil, Cuba, Chile, El Salvador, Guatemala, Honduras, Mexico, and Peru. Since 2008, he has lived in Mexico where he teaches, and directs a small literary press called Santa Muerte cartonera. He holds a doctorate in literature with a focus in art theory.

Oliver Welden (Santiago, 1946) is an award-winning poet from Chile. In 1968, he received the Luis Tello National Poetry Award of the Society of Chilean Writers for *Perro del Amor*, a collection of 23 of his poems. In the 1960s, Welden and his wife also published a poetry journal in Chile called *Tebaida (Thebes)*.

Rodrigo Verdugo was born in Santiago de Chile on January 9, 1977. Co-editor and columnist of the Journal Stroke. Member of the Surrealist Group Stroke. Sub director of Editions Stroke. Sub director and co-editor Rayentru Journal Magazine labia minora. It began in the Poetry Workshop "Isla Negra" led by the poet Edmundo Herrera from 1922 to 1996 in the Sech. His work has been published in magazines and anthologies in Chile and abroad being partly translated into French, Italian, Portuguese, Polish and Arabic. In 2002 he published his first book "Knots veiled" Ed Spill In 2005 participates in the exhibition "Southern Cone Spill or travel of the Argonauts"at the Fundación Eugenio Granell (Santiago de Compostela, Spain) and won first place in the competition "Wings of Poetry" organized by the Friends of Poetry "(Monterrey. Mexico). In 2008 he participated in the International Exhibition of Surrealism

"0 back do Olhar"at the Casa de la Cultura de Coimbra (Coimbra, Portugal) and in 2009 participated in the International Exhibition of Surrealism "Iluminacoes discontinued " at the Convent of San José, (Lagoa, Portugal).

Ramón Sepúlveda lives in Canada since 1974. His short stories have been published in anthologies in Canada, Unites States, Mexico, the Dominican Republic and Chile, such as *Chilean Literature in Canada*, Naín Nómez, 1981, *Northern Cronopios : Chilean novelists and short story writers in Canada*, an anthology edited, with an introduction by Jorge Etcheverry and *Cruzando la cordillera, el cuento chileno 1973-1983*, de Armando Epple. His book of short stories *Red Rock* was first published in Canada in 1990, and its Spanish version in Chile in 1991. One of his short stories is part of the English textbook *Pens of Many Colours*, published by Seneca College, Toronto, 1998. He was one of the founding members of *Ediciones Cordillera*, a publishing house of Chilean exiled writers in Ottawa. He is also one of the Directors of *Red Cultural Hispánica*, an organization tat promotes and facilitates the hispanic culture and literature written in Canada.

Gabriela Etcheverry is a Chilean-Canadian writer and promoter of cultural events. She has a PhD from Laval University and two Master's degrees from Carleton University, where she taught for many years. In 2007 she published the novel *Latitudes*, a French version of which will be published by Antares (Toronto) early in 2011. She published a bilingual illustrated book for children, *Añañuca*, in 2010. A story from her collection "You and Me" was awarded the first prize in the 5th annual national short story contest "Nuestra palabra" (2008). Works from "The Breadfruit Tree and Other Stories" and "You and Me" have appeared, along with poems, in anthologies, magazines, and cultural supplements. Extracts from her short novels *El regreso, Guayacán: tesoro y lujuria, Where Are You?* and *Alejandra* can be found in www.qantatilterario.com and www.revistaqantati.com.

D. Álvar de Castro is the pseudonym used by David Castro Rubio. David was born in Santiago, Chile, in 1957. He immigrated to Canada in 1974. The experiences of integration and cultural adaptation are explored in his books *Cleo*, Canada, Ponce Editores, 2003 and *By This River*, Canada, Per Mor Press, 2010. He is thus of a younger generation of Chilean-Canadian writers and poets who were university students or established activists and artists when the coup occurred. The combination of his Chilean and Quebec experiences have made him a man of three cultures, who writes fluently in both Spanish and English. In this sense, he's both a multilingual or polylingual writer and a poet who is able to play with languages and the interface between them, inhabiting his own unique interlinguistic and intercultural space. His poetry has appeared in anthologies and magazines in Spanish and English.

Alejandro Raúl Mujica-Olea was born in Santiago, Chile on August 8, 1947. He became a political refugee in Edmonton. Alejandro has completed five books of poetry, two of which have been translated into English. His poetry has been published in Nightline, Unicorns Be, Sigla, La Voz, Entrelineas, Voyage Prensa Latina, Horizontes and The New Orphic Review and has also been read over the radio of the University of Victoria and the University of Washington as well as the Co-op Radio in Vancouver. Alejandro's poetry has received several awards in the United States and Canada. He co founder of *The World Poetry Series* at the Vancouver Public Library and World Poetry Café a Radio Show on Co-op Radio 102.7 FM," a multicultural venue, with more than 300 participating poets of all ethnic backgrounds.

Jorge Nef. Born in Santiago, Chile in 1942; in Canada since 1975. Studied in Chile and did postgraduate studies in Political Science at Vanderbilt University, the University of California at Santa Barbara and the Latin American Faculty of Social Sciences. He has participated in numerous international conferences and was Canadian Delegate to the South Commission (Geneva 1989), and worked as a consultant and/or cooperant for the IDRC, CIDA and the Pan American Health

Organization. Currently, DR. Nef is Professor Emeritus at the University of Guelph. He has written edited and co-edited 16 books on political and international issues, and over 120 scholarly articles in refereed journals and in books on issues of human security, technology and democracy. *La region perdida* (Madrid, Betania 1997) is his first poetry book. His poems appeared in *Alter Vox* (2000), *Poetas sin fronteras* (Madrid: Verbum, 2000, ed. Ramiro Lagos), *Boreal* (Ottawa: Split Quotation, 2001, eds. Jorge Etcheverry and Luciano Díaz), *Boreal 1 Antología: Poetas de Chile en Canadá*, CD (2004), the *International Poetry Review* (2004), *La voz y la memoria. Antología de la poesia chilena en Canada* (Luis Torres and Luciano Diaz, 2009) and in *Antares 2009* (Ed. Margarita Feliciano).

Julio Piñones was born in Antofagasta in 1948. He holds a degree as a professor with a specialization in Spanish Language and Literature (University of Chile, 1973) and a doctorate in Spanish American Literature (Universidad Complutense, Madrid, 1990). Currently, he is teaching Theory and Literary Aesthetics at the University of La Serena. In the 1960s he published poems in such literary magazines as *Humboldt* (Germany), *El Rehilete* (Mexico City) and *Taller Literario* (Havana). In 1970 and 1987 received prizes for unpublished books from the Municipality of Santiago and the Chilean Writers' Association. The *Consejo Nacional del Libro y la Lectura* awarded him the "A la trayectoria en el campo de las letras" scholarship in 1997. In 2004, on the occasion of the centenary of the birth of Pablo Neruda, he was awarded the Presidential Medal of Honour. He published his first book of poems, *Andadura* (Valdivia), in 1982; other collections followed: *Poemares* (La Serena, 1991); *Pecados cordiales* (Valdivia, 1994); *Bellas y orates* (2000); and *Travesía* (2008). He was a member of the School of Santiago, a Chilean avant-garde poetry group of late 1960s and early1970s. His work has appeared in numerous anthologies: *Orfeo* (1968); *Literatura Chilena, Creación y Crítica* (1983), *Poesía nueva de Chile* (California, 1983); and *En el ojo del huracán* (1991). He has published scholarly papers, essays and literary studies in specialized journals.

Verónica Jiménez (Santiago of Chile, 1964). She is a journalist with a degree in Literature. She has published *Floating Islands* (Stratis, 1998) and *Hex Words* (2002). She has been anthologized in: *Codices. Poetry anthology*, RIL, Santiago, 1994; *young Chilean poets*, Ediciones LAR, Concepción, 1997, *Anthology of Young Chilean Poetry*, Editorial Universitaria, Santiago, first edition 1999, second edition 2003; *anthology of erotic poetry*, Chile, Lom Ediciones, Santiago, 2000; *Altira. Sample of Chilean poetry*, Ediciones Vox, Buenos Aires, 2001; and *Nineteen Chilean Poets of the Nineties*, J.C. Sáez Editor, Santiago, 2006.

Fernando Rubilar (Santiago of Chile, 1973). Formal studies of Plastic Arts at the University of Chile for 4 years. Further inroads in the Contemporary Dance Company belonging to the DEMO. He has participated in poetry workshops with Gonzalo Millán, Edmundo Herrera and Raul Zurita. He has published the poetry book *Farewell to suicidal poets* in 2003. Has been selected for Latin America Writer's Anthology 2006 Alternative Root editorial, Argentina.

Víctor Sáez .Born in Santiago of Chile the year 1962. Licensed in Philosophy. With residence in diverse countries for almost a decade in the 80s.He is the author of *To Read Under the Rain* and *Provisional Inventory*.

Sergio Castillo Arrau. Chilean writer with residence in Peru. Professor and playwright director. He have written books and plays.

Rafael Pulgar Hills (Valparaíso, Chile 1970) has published *Las Flores del Ocio* (RIL, 2002) and *Meridiano Percepción, Odisea del Poeta Imaginario*. (Andrómeda, 2007). He is a writer, poet, publicist and Professor of Creative Redaction and Semiotic in Chilean Universities.

Magdalena Fuentes Zurita. Born in Los Angeles, Chile, she is a poet, researcher of popular culture and has served as a monitor of literary workshops. During 2006-2007 she was General Secretary of

the Chilean Writers Society. Magdalena Fuentes Zurita's work has appeared in numerous anthologies and literary magazines, including /
Poetry From Chile: 26 New Voices/ (University of California, 1993), and
/*Literastur*/ (Spain, 2003).

Bilingual writer **Carmen Rodríguez** left Chile following the 1973 military coup and made her home in Vancouver, Canada. She is the award-winning author of *Guerra prolongada/Protracted War*, a volume of poetry, and *De cuerpo entero/and a body to remember with*, a short story collection. Rodríguez teaches in the Latin American Studies Program of Simon Fraser University and is the Vancouver correspondent for the Spanish Section of Radio Canada International.

Gabriel Larenas was born is Santiago Chile, 1982. He graduated from Aesthetics and English Literature at the Catholic University of Chile. He is currently doing his M.A. in Cultural Studies at the Arcis University of Chile. He was recently featured in the *Plaza Baquedano* Anthology by Mago Publishing House; a small compilation that publishes new fiction writers and poets. He is currently working in his first poetry book.

Lautaro Ramos Guerra , Chilean, 57 years, professor . He has published more than 15 books on Literature and education . He obtained more than 20 national and international literary prizes .He is director of "Rising," the literary factory of the city of Algarrobo, Chile. And organizing manager of the Recent Literary contest "Ecritos in Napkins of paper", event that reunited more than a thousand writers of Chile and Ibero-America.

Humberto Gatica was born and educated in Chile. His poetry has been published in magazine magazines like: *Cauce* (Chile); *Callao* (Perú); *Poetry Wales*; *Blithe Spirit*; *Still*; *Exiled Writers* (United Kingdom) Anthologies :*Haiku*. Poetry Ancient and Modern; *Between*

A Mountain And The Sea (2003); *Soft Touch* (2005); *Festival Of The Wolf* (2006).He lives and works in Swansea, Wales, United Kingdom.

Víctor Sepúlveda Carrasco (1954) Atacama, Chile. He works as a philosophy teacher. He writes essays, poetry, as well as narrative and historical novellas. He has won numerous literary prices. His works has been published in diverse anthologies in Spain, Argentina and Peru.

Zulema Retamal. Chilean poet and storyteller. Professor of Spanish at the University of Concepción. She belongs to the Society of Writers of Chile (Sech). She has published poetry collections and *The Strokes moon that we are not holy* (Ril editores, 2002) and the novel *Facedor of Pages* in 2005. In 2003 she received the Creative Writing Fellowship from the National Book Council. Participate as speaker at international congresses of literature conducted in Chile, Hungary, Peru and Spain.

Juan Garrido-Salgado was born in Chile. He was a political prisoner under the Pinochet regime, but now lives in Adelaide (Australia). He has published four books of poetry and many poems in magazines in Chile, Colombia, Spain, and Australia. He translated 5 aboriginal poets into Spanish for the Anthology Espejo de Tierra/ Earth Mirror; Aboriginal and Mapuche poets published in Australia, 2008; Currently working in his new book: *Mirror of Two Souls*.

Luis Correa-Díaz is Professor of Spanish at The University of Georgia (http://www.rom.uga.edu) He is the author of *Cervantes y/en (las) Américas: mapa de campo y ensayo de bibliografía razonada* (2006), *Una historia apócrifa de América: el arte de la conjetura histórica de Pedro Gómez Valderrama* (2003), *Todas las muertes de Pinochet: Notas literarias para una biografía crítica* (2000), and *Lengua muerta: Poesía, post-literatura & erotismo en Enrique Lihn* (1996). Co-editor (with Silvia Nagy-Zekmi) of *Arte de vivir: acercamientos críticos a la poesía de Pedro Lastra* (2007). His poetry books are: *Cosmological Me* (forthcoming), *Mester de soltería* (2006/2008), *Diario de un poeta recién divorciado*

(2005), *Divina Pastora* (1998), *Rosario de actos de habla* (1993), *Ojo de buey* (1993), and *Bajo la pequeña música de su pie* (1990).

Violeta Brana-Lafourcade. Born in Montreal in 1981. Her parents, both Chilean, fled from the military dictatorship of Pinochet. Violeta moved to New York at the age of six and later to Germany as a teenager. She took her M.A. in American Literature and Film Studies at Johannes-Gutenberg University in Mainz, Germany. Currently, she is living in Madrid, where she continues to write and has also directed several short films.

Paulina Ramírez was born in Santiago, Chile in 1965 and resides with her husband in Boston, MA. Paulina is completing studies in Writing, Literature and Publishing at Emerson College in Boston. *The Impact of September* is the first in a series of poems about the journey of self-discovery that began with a trip to Chile in 1989. She is also writing a memoir of her experience as an immigrant child raised in America. Paulina is a permanent resident of the United States and retains her Chilean citizenship.

Bernardo E. Navia was born in Chillán (Chile) in 1967. The oldest brother of four children, he had the opportunity to live and to study in several countries (Perú, Argentina, and Puerto Rico among them.) Presently, he lives in Chicago where he works as an Associate Professor for DePaul University. He is married to Leslie Klatt. Together they have two sons: Inti and Leaf.

Renato Martínez, was born in Santiago, Chile, in 1943, he moved to US in 1978 as a consequence of the 1973 coup d'état in his country. He studied at the University of Chile first and then at the University of California in San Diego, where he obtained a Ph. D. in Literature. He is presently an instructor at the City College of Fresno, California, and he has published poetry and critical articles in different magazines and books.

Teresa Gónzalez-Lee. She is a poet. This, she owes to public school teachers who, in the spirit of Gabriela Mistral, auspiciously prepared their young students for Children's Literary Contests. A near death experience, years later, rekindled her poetic craft. She's been a bilingual poet, teaching and publishing in English and Spanish. Her poems appear in academic anthologies, cultural magazines and online.

M. Galician is pseudonym of Manuel M. Olmos. He is a Canadian citizen, originally from Chile. In his country he started writing poetry and short stories. In Toronto he contributed articles to *Jornada*, a Latin-american community newspaper and recently he finished a book of poetry titled *La Memoria Invicta (The unconquered memory)* and a book of testimonies entitled *Nosotros los de Entonces (We, of those times)*.

Víctor Olivares Andreani. Born in Valparaiso, Chile and living in Montreal Canada. He is a mechanical designer and writes poetry.

Pablo Paredes. Poet and Playwright, he is a professor at the University of Santiago with a masters in Political Communication from the University of Chile. His published poetry includes "Frío en la Noche Latina" (*Cold in the Latino Night*) Santiago 2004, "El Final de la Fiesta" (*The End of the Party*) Santiago 2005, "El Niño Dios" (*The God Child*) Mexico City 2006, "Mi Hijo Down" (*My Son Down*) Buenos Aires 2008 and "La Raza Chilena" (*The Chilean Race*) Montevideo 2010. He is the director of the Ibo-American Festival of Current Poetry "Poquita Fe" (*Little Faith*). His theater showcases include the adaptation of "Desdicha Obrera, una tijera clavada en el corazón" (*Miserable Working Woman, a Scissors Stuck in the Heart* -2007), original work by Luís Emilio Recabarren: father of the Chilean labor movement. "Meri Crismas, Peñi" (2008), "ABC1" (2009) a critical portrait of the new Chilean upper class co-written with Begoña Ugalde, "Las enfermitas Sagradas de Chile" (*The Sacred Little Sick Girls of Chile* -2009), "Jorge González Murió" (*Jorge González Died*

-2009). Most recently he showcased "Las Analfabetas" (*The Illiterates*), "La Vida es Sueño" (*Live is Dream*) with poems and new scenes, "Ángel a Martillazos" (*Hammering Angel* -2011), and the Belgian/Chilean co-production of "Historia Abierta" (*Open History*). His texts have been translated to English, Portuguese and German.

www.ingramcontent.com/pod-product-compliance
Lightning Source LLC
LaVergne TN
LVHW011416080426
835512LV00005B/90